DISCARD

Old World, New Horizons

The Godkin Lectures at Harvard University
1967

The Godkin Lectures on the Essentials of Free Government and the Duties of the Citizen were established at Harvard University in 1903 in memory of Edwin Lawrence Godkin (1831-1902). They are given annually under the auspices of the John Fitzgerald Kennedy School of Government.

Old World, New Horizons

Britain, Europe, and the Atlantic Alliance

Edward Heath

Harvard University Press

Cambridge, Massachusetts

1970

Contents

Introduction

The lectures which follow were delivered at Harvard in March 1967. They were an attempt to look behind the immediate headlines and examine in greater depth the stage which Europe had reached in its search for unity. I was particularly concerned to trace the development of the European Economic Community and to deduce from its history the direction of its future development. At the same time I examined Britain's attitude towards the EEC and how British aspirations in Europe fitted into a general concept of Britain's place in the world.

It would have been normal for these lectures to be published within a few months of delivery. But when almost immediately the British Government announced its intention of making a fresh application for membership of the EEC it seemed to me that interest would concentrate on the outcome of these negotiations. For the delay in publication which has occurred I therefore take entire responsibility. When it was suggested in the middle of 1969 that the lectures might still be published, my first reaction was that the passage of time might have outdated them to such an extent that they would only be worth reproducing if extensive changes were made. But having reread the lectures I concluded that they should stand as they were delivered and that they still contained the main elements of my thinking about Europe.

Much has happened since March 1967, but insofar as they concern Europe, events have in a curious way brought us full circle. Now, as in 1967, we in Europe are in the middle of a lively debate about our future. This debate has two main facets. It is partly a debate throughout our continent on the meaning and content of the search for European unity. It is partly a debate within Britain on the likelihood and wisdom of Britain's entry into the EEC and on the effect which such entry would have upon our future prosperity, security, and national identity. The previous debate in 1967 fizzled out without making much advance. The second British attempt to enter the EEC failed even before negotiations began. The EEC itself, while completing the tariff union and working hard to consolidate a common agricultural policy, has not yet advanced far beyond these bounds to establish an economic union or to lay foundations for harmonising foreign and defence policies. The question now is whether the current debate will be equally unproductive or whether it will eventually recreate the momentum which Europe so badly needs.

I am sure that the answer to these questions will depend on our clarity of thought as well as our energy in action. The time has gone when simple eloquence on the theme of unity can produce useful results either in Britain or on the Continent. These lectures are put forward as a possible contribution to such clarity of thought. In this preface I shall attempt very briefly to set out how recent events have affected the analysis both as regards Europe as a whole and the particular question of Britain's relationship with it.

The second attempt by the British Government to enter the EEC in 1967 will probably come to be regarded as a minor curiosity of European diplomatic history. Since President de Gaulle had made it clear when imposing his veto in 1963 that he acted on general political grounds, and since his power of veto still remained in 1967, it seemed obvious that British entry could only be achieved under one of two hypotheses. The first was that contrary to all his public statements, President de Gaulle had relaxed his political objection. The alternative hypothesis was that even though he maintained his objection, his five partners in the EEC, and in particular Germany, could be mobilised to persuade or force him to abandon it. To the outside observer, neither of these hypotheses seemed tenable at any time during the discussions of 1967. The second hypothesis, on which the British Government seemed mainly to rely, stemmed in my view from a misunderstanding of the nature of the EEC and in particular of the relationship between France and Germany.

This is not the place to enter into the details of this argument. It is enough to say that the attempt of 1967 had two consequences in Britain, one positive, the other negative. The positive result was that for the first time the Labour Party became committed to British membership of the EEC with its implications for the future unity of Europe. As a result the House of Commons in May 1967 approved this policy by an overwhelming majority in which the leadership of all three parties participated.

The negative result was that the second failure began to sour British opinion towards the whole enterprise. It was natural that many people should begin to be less interested in a Community which had twice rebuffed them. This disinterest was increased by the apparent stagnation of the Community itself, which began to lose some of the glamour earned by its previous achievements.

This situation continued more or less unchanged through 1968 and the first part of 1969. Nevertheless during this time events of the highest importance to Europe made it clear that the underlying need for European unity was becoming more pressing.

One of these events was the Soviet invasion of Czechoslovakia. This showed that the Soviet Union was still prepared to use force to defend interests which could only be defined as essential by a brutal use of logic. It was noticeable that the Soviet invasion produced a stronger reaction in Western Europe than in the United States. It coincided with, and only briefly arrested, a growing reluctance of the United States to continue carrying so heavy a weight of responsibility for the defence of her allies. In the third of my Godkin Lectures, I described the implications for Europe of this growing impatience with the burdens which history had thrust upon the United States. The harrowing experience of the United States in Vietnam has inevitably affected the American attitude towards the defence of Europe. At a time when Soviet action has made it clear to all except the blindest that European defence cannot safely be neglected, the inevitable conclusion is that the countries of Europe must learn to do more to protect themselves.

In my Godkin Lectures I was led by this train of thought to propose that the British and French nuclear forces should be pooled to form a joint deterrent which would be held in trust for Europe. I later suggested that this could be achieved by setting up a European Group which would be given in relation to the joint Anglo-French force the same functions as the so-called McNamara Committee in the North Atlantic Treaty Organisation exercises towards the United States nuclear deterrent today. This arrangement would not involve a breach of the non-proliferation treaty since it would not involve giving control over nuclear weapons to non-nuclear powers. So, far from involving a break with the United States or NATO, this proposal could provide a means for healing the breach which at present exists between France and her NATO allies.

I have never argued that this proposal is in some way a condition of British membership of the EEC. I believe however that it would provide part of the answer to the wider question of the future defence of Europe. For this reason I have urged that the British Government should be ready to discuss such ideas with the French and other European Governments. I have been encouraged to find that the same proposal or variations of it have recently begun to find favour among influential opinion on both sides of the English Channel.

The other main pressure on Europe since 1967 has been in the monetary field. Sterling was devalued eight months after I delivered my lectures. It is still at the time of writing too early to pass a final verdict on the success of devaluation in righting the British balance of payments more than temporarily. Certainly its effects have been more complicated and slow-acting than most of its proponents then predicted. The devaluation of sterling gave a shock to the sterling system and so sharpened the problem of the sterling balances which I dealt with in the second of my lectures. The Basle Agreement of 1968 represented an international attempt to bring under control a situation which the British Government no longer had the resources to handle. In this arrangement the other countries of Europe played a major part. Britain would have gained considerable political as well as financial benefit if she had agreed to discuss such arrangements in 1967, as I suggested in my lecture.

At the same time a wider uncertainty persists in monetary matters as a result of the increase in Britain's indebtedness, the continued deficit of the United States, the devaluation of the franc, and the tendency of Germany to run a trading surplus. This uncertainty goes wider than Europe and raises the whole question of whether the world's main trading countries can find a more satisfactory source of international liquidity than a persistent American deficit creating an unregulated flow of dollars to Europe through the Euro-dollar market.

These pressures in favour of new action in bringing together policies of European countries were clear when the change of President in France took place. At the time of writing it is too soon to be sure how far President Pompidou and his Government will be flexible either in discussing fresh progress within the EEC itself or in agreeing to negotiations with the countries which have applied for membership. It is already certain that there will be no sharp reversal of policy and that the French Government will continue as before resolutely to defend its own conception of the French national interest. The handling of the devaluation of the franc made this plain enough. It seems probable that the French Government will insist on a clearer definition of policy within the existing Community, particularly in the field of agriculture, before agreeing to allow negotiations for the entry of applicant members.

This prospect involves a paradox for those in Britain who favour eventual British entry into the EEC. On the one hand, if the Community gathers speed and begins once again to progress towards economic and political union it will inevitably make fresh arrangements and develop fresh institutions to which Britain will then be asked to adhere without having had any say in their formation. On the other hand, a stagnant Community has proved increasingly unattractive to British opinion.

This is not the occasion to set out the tactics which I think the British Government ought to follow in these circumstances. I believe that the analysis in these lectures, made before the attempt in 1967, is still broadly valid for an attempt in 1970 or thereafter. This must be seen as a great enterprise demanding farsightedness and patience. A third failure might have a very serious effect. The need for careful preparation in advance of any formal negotiations is even more obvious than it was in 1967. So is the importance of extending these preparations to cover subjects which do not fall immediately within the scope of the Treaty of Rome. As I have tried to show it is precisely in these fields, for example in defence and monetary matters, that the recent pressures on Europe have been most intense.

At the same time there is the need, both in Britain and on the Continent, to recover in public opinion the ground which has admittedly been lost during the years of stagnation. This can only be done by setting out the prospects honestly and showing that when we talk about the unity of Europe we mean not a vague concept, but the habit of working together to reach accepted goals. If I had to sum up the theme of these three lectures in one sentence it would be that this habit of working together is the essence of a Community; it is the only foundation on which the unity of Europe can be built.

In the last of my lectures at Harvard I described the stance which I thought Europe should take towards the world outside. I have always believed that it was wide of the mark to criticise the movement towards European Unity on the grounds that it was encouraging Europe to look inwards on itself. To me one of the main justifications of this movement has been that it would equip Europe to play a more worthwhile part in the outside world. As the countries of Europe availed themselves of the benefits of co-operation they would be able to make a more effective contribution not only to the prosperity of the countries of Asia and Africa and Latin America but also to the political stability without which prosperity is an illusion.

So far as Britain is concerned there has been a set-back since I lectured at Harvard. In January 1968, the British Government decided that regardless of its commitments or the turn of political events, it would withdraw all British forces from the Arabian Gulf and from Singapore/Malaysia by the end of 1971. It is clear that the decision was taken in a hurry without any serious assessment of its effect in these areas. It brought to a head a debate which had been carried on for some years about the role of Britain overseas. In some ways this debate ran parallel to a similar debate which has been conducted in the United States.

In both these countries this debate poses the basic question to what extent, if at all, Britain and the United States or indeed the other countries of the West should be called upon to help maintain a framework of basic stability in the world within which change can be peacefully achieved. It may be true that in the past British and American Governments have assumed almost automatically a readiness to come to the help of friends in distress. There have been occasions since World War II when efforts of this kind have been ill-conceived and unsuccessful. But I am certain that it would be quite wrong to deduce from these experiences that it will never be in our interest to make such efforts again.

Of course it would be greatly preferable if this essential framework of stability could be achieved by the United Nations. Failing that, it is certainly desirable that the countries of each region should achieve among themselves the necessary balance within which they can develop their own societies in their own way. But we must recognise that in the world as we see it today, neither of these conditions obtains. There will be occasions in the future, as in the past, when friendly countries will ask Britain or the United States to help them to cope with an external threat to their stability. Such appeals will always confront our Governments with a difficult choice. I believe that it would be as stupid to assume that such appeals should always be rejected as to assume that they should always be acted upon. The decision should depend in each case on the political context.

It happens that British forces have in the past operated in the Gulf and in Singapore/Malaysia in a way which has proved politically acceptable in the area. The political context has been right and Britain has been able, without antagonising the citizens of these countries, to help their governments cope with external threats which would otherwise have made nonsense of any hope of peaceful progress. In my judgment this is a limited effort which Britain could and should maintain in co-operation with our friends. I would fully endorse the conclusion which President Nixon reached when he told the people of Thailand: "Our determination to honor our commitments is fully consistent with our conviction that the nations of Asia can and must increasingly shoulder the responsibility for achieving peace and progress in the area. The challenge to our wisdom is to support the Asian countries' efforts to defend and develop themselves, without attempting to take from them the responsibilities which should be theirs. For if domination by the aggressor can destroy the freedom of a nation, too much dependence on a protector can eventually erode its dignity."

Of course, as I tried to make clear in my third lecture, this British argument is only part of a wider picture. It is natural that, in the immediate aftermath of empire, the countries of continental Europe should be reluctant once again to expose themselves to rebuffs overseas. It is natural that while Europe is still half-made the problems of Europe should loom largest in their consciousness. But in the long run Europe will either be outward-looking or it will be nothing. The interests of Europe overseas are already so great that they are bound to have an effect on the course of European policies. The countries of Europe have been inclined to take it for granted that the United States, and in particular areas Britain and France, will provide the essential framework of stability within which their affairs can prosper. We are now, I believe, not far from the point where it will be obvious that those who expect to benefit from this stability must be prepared to make a contribution to its continuance.

EDWARD HEATH

London
September 19, 1969

I The Growing Pains of the New Europe

On the twelfth of December 1826 George Canning, then Her Majesty's principal Secretary of State for Foreign Affairs, spoke these memorable words in the House of Commons: "I called the New World into existence to redress the balance of the Old." He was defending the support England had given to the people of South America rebelling against the authority of a Spanish Empire that had itself come under the domination of France. Now, just over 140 years later, my theme reverses the old proposition. It is that the Old World must now be brought together to redress the balance of the New, that we must try to create a wider unity between the ancient nation states of Europe, of which Britain must be a part, so that together we can provide the basis for a better balance with our friends and allies on this side of the Atlantic. In so doing we can make sure that as the disparity between the two sides diminishes so the possibility of the formation of a real Atlantic Community is brought closer.

There have been three motive forces behind the desire for a greater European unity.

First, the determination to put an end once and for all to the nationalist rivalry and internecine warfare which has ravaged Europe for so long, brought desperate suffering to her people, and almost destroyed her culture and civilisation.

Secondly, the recognition that for the new generation the attitudes of mind and the hopes and aspirations which unite them are far greater than the nationalist feelings which divide them. For them national boundaries have little meaning. The teenager in Frankfurt has the same feelings and ambitions as the youngster in Manchester.

Thirdly, the desire to benefit from production and marketing in a larger economic market and to develop technology on a genuinely European scale. Unless this is achieved the European nations must reconcile themselves to the fact that they will remain forever second-class industrial powers.

This is an opportune moment at which to discuss these motive forces. There is a feeling of change in the air. There is also a sense of confusion, tinged sometimes with disillusion and even cynicism. People in the West have a feeling that the clear sense of direction which they once possessed — whether it was in support of the Atlantic Alliance when confronted with the obvious threat from the Warsaw Pact, or whether it was in the strong and sturdy movement towards closer European unity — has been lost. The momentum inside Europe appears to have weakened. And externally the preoccupation of the United States with the war in Vietnam gives the impression across the Atlantic of a lack of American interest in European policies. Indeed the war in Vietnam itself blurs the impression of progress towards a detente between the United States and Soviet Russia, between the Atlantic Alliance and the Warsaw Pact, just at a time when the antipathy between Communist China and the Soviet Union, combined with the convulsions inside China itself, might have been expected greatly to assist the lessening of tension between the Western and Eastern powers.

The United States, through every administration, has given unstinted support to the development of the European Economic Community. It has never hidden its belief that it would like to see it widened to embrace other states, in particular Britain. It has every right to be proud of the rapid growth in prosperity, and consequently in stability, of those European countries which it so generously aided in the late forties and the fifties. At the same time the United States has sometimes seemed to me to lack an understanding of what that Europeanism, which it has so greatly encouraged, really means today; of what the consequences are of this growth of European feeling combined with economic and financial strength, consequences in particular for the United States. And perhaps none of us has really quite grasped the consequent need to redress the balance in trade and commerce, in finance, in political organisation, and in defence between the two sides of the Atlantic.

Each of these factors can be treated and discussed in isolation, but there is perhaps behind them all a more general feeling. It is now just over twenty-one years since the end of the Second World War, in which all of the powers and all of the continents I have mentioned were involved. A complete generation has come of age since then. It knew nothing of the War or its background, it took no part in it, and it does not feel itself in any way committed to its consequences. And having come of age it is pervaded by a mood of questioning, individually and nationally; questioning the purpose and direction of each individual life; questioning the object and the reason for each national existence itself. In many ways this is healthy if it drives us back to first principles, and leads us to re-establish a firm basis for future policies.

It is just at this time that the British Government is making a renewed approach towards membership of the European Economic Community. This must be seen against the long background of the attempt to establish a viable British European policy. It is useful at this stage to examine some of the landmarks in Britain's relations with Europe since the War, not in order to write history but to pinpoint the lessons to be learnt from the past.

The theme of a greater European unity has absorbed the interests and energies of numberless people both in Europe and America ever since the end of the Second World War. It was Winston Churchill who, in his speech at Zurich just over twenty years ago, issued the clarion call for Europe to unite.

I well recall, one day in 1962, when I was immersed in the negotiations for Britain's entry into the European Community, the British Broadcasting Corporation telephoned me at the Foreign Office in London to say that they had discovered in their archives a tape recording which they had not previously known existed, a recording of that speech of Winston Churchill at Zurich. Would I like it played over to me? I eagerly accepted this invitation. They brought the recording to the Foreign Office where the other members of the British delegation and myself gathered round the tape recorder to hear it played back. I shall never forget the feelings of exhilaration with which I heard that powerful voice come back over the years, unmistakable in its resonance, and I shall always prize the intense feeling of purpose which it gave us. "I am now going to say something" he declared "that will astonish you. The first step in the re-creation of the European family must be a partnership between France and Germany. In this way only can France recover the moral leadership of Europe. There can be no revival of Europe without a spiritually great France and a spiritually great Germany". That was not only a farseeing declaration; it was one of immense courage less than eighteen months after the end of a long and bitter war.

In this speech Mr. Churchill outlined the sort of Europe which he visualised. It was a Europe to be based on the rapprochement between France and Germany around which the other European countries would congregate. This was to be one of the three great groupings of the world. The others were to be the United States and the British Commonwealth and Empire as it then was. From this pattern several points emerged. First he believed that a united Europe could only be soundly based on a partnership between France and Germany. How right he was. Yet in practice whenever these two powers have seemed to be coming closer together there has been much soul-searching not only in Britain and the smaller European countries, but also in the United States itself. The closer relationship between General de Gaulle and Chancellor Adenauer, for example, which culminated in the signing of the Franco-German Treaty in Paris in 1963, brought back anxieties about a Franco-German domination of Europe. And yet whenever these two countries have drifted apart, as they have done over recent years, there has been an even greater tension in Europe, a tension which in its turn has affected the work of the European Economic Community.

There are some who constantly urge us to use the political argument that Britain should become a member of the Community in order to support France in withstanding growing German pressure. At the time of the last negotiations this was never an effective argument for the simple reason that the French people believed they were perfectly capable themselves of containing any German power in the foreseeable future. The fact that Germany was a divided country and likely to remain so for some time to come had its psychological impact on the force and clarity with which German policy could be carried through in Europe. Moreover the French believed that their own rising population, with a new tough generation coming of age, would be fully able to handle this situation. This therefore was not at the time an effective argument to try to bring to bear on the French. It is possible that in this regard circumstances today are changing. At the same time it is quite clear that the other powers of Europe and in particular the smaller countries would welcome Britain's accession to the Community to remove any anxiety they might feel about this partnership.

I myself always agreed with Mr. Churchill's view that there is undoubted advantage to Europe in having an accord between France and Germany. I therefore wanted to see the Franco-German Treaty operated successfully. For reasons which are well-known this proved difficult at the highest levels in the last German Government under Dr. Erhard, though the Treaty appeared to operate well at the lower levels both on the military and civil sides. I am glad to see that the policy of the grand coalition in the German Federal Republic is to work more closely with France through this Treaty. At the same time I am sure that Britain has a vital part to play in any political arrangements which may develop inside the Community in helping to provide a broader basis than a purely bilateral one for a future European entity.

Secondly, Mr. Churchill visualised that some of the Eastern Socialist states might become members of the United Europe for which he was calling, though he held out little hope of a European unity stretching from the Atlantic to the Urals or beyond. But today when we hear in Europe the call for Yalta to be rewritten and for Europe to be created, East and West as well as North and South, it is well to recall his original conception.

Thirdly, he did not see Britain as a member of this United Europe. Britain and the Commonwealth and Empire were themselves to be one powerful world grouping. Later on he was to develop this into his concept of Britain at the heart of three concentric circles, the centre of the Commonwealth and Empire, geographically and historically a part of Europe and through ties of blood and common interest closely allied to North America. In his concept of the place to be filled by the Commonwealth grouping he failed to foresee the development of the Empire as it then was into a large number of independent states, formally connected only by the Sovereign as head of the Commonwealth. Whereas Europe was coming more closely together politically, the growing numbers of the members of the Commonwealth were pursuing more and more independent policies.

To sum up, for Mr. Churchill there was to be a United — and be it noted Federal — Europe on the mainland for whom the United States and the British Commonwealth and, he hoped, the Soviet Union, were to be the sponsors.

Nine months after Winston Churchill's speech at Zurich, General Marshall, then United States Secretary of State, put forward at Harvard in June 1947 the most magnanimous offer yet made by one country to another: to help the European states to rebuild their prosperity if they would co-operate together in the work they were doing. It was Ernest Bevin, then British Foreign Secretary, who speedily led the response to that offer, a response which almost included some of the Eastern Socialist states. Looking back we can see how much closer we would have come to a true European unity — not only North and South but East as well as West — if Poland and Czechoslovakia, to mention only two, had been able to join in that movement towards European economic co-operation. How much easier our task would be today. But the Iron Curtain had fallen, an Iron Curtain to which Winston Churchill had already called the attention of the world at Fulton, Missouri, some fifteen months earlier. The gap in Europe between West and East still remains unbridged.

Soon the countries of Western Europe were making progress in diverse ways towards a closer relationship. At the Council of Europe in Strasbourg they were able to discuss political problems of common interest. Indeed, they were able to go further. They could negotiate conventions between themselves to provide a common basis on which to work and to facilitate a freer interchange between their citizens. In Paris, the Organisation for European Economic Co-operation was doing the same work in the economic field. And when NATO was formed the European countries co-operated with North America in their own defence.

But for some, these efforts at co-operative arrangements were inadequate to meet the real requirements of the second half of the twentieth century. In particular, the Six — France, Italy, Germany, Belgium, the Netherlands, and Luxembourg — all of whom had at some time during the Second World War been vanquished and overrun, felt that the old form of nation state had failed them and that the new form of co-operative organisation, though far in advance of anything that had previously existed, was still unable to provide the common framework in which they could restore their shattered economies, rebuild their bombed cities, and provide a better standard of living for their people. Thus it was that the Six came together and created in 1950–1951 first the Coal and Steel Community, to be followed in 1966–1968 by Euratom and the European Economic Community, a process of institutional development in which Britain alas played no part.

The debate on the Schuman Plan for creating the Coal and Steel Community took place in the House of Commons soon after I was first elected to Parliament. In my maiden speech on 26 June 1950 I urged the then Labour Government to accept the invitation to join the talks on the same basis as the Netherlands Government, accepting the ultimate objective but without prior commitment to the final outcome. At that stage Britain could have played her part in shaping the future development of European unity. After being the home of the European Governments in exile during the War and after being so prominent in the organisations for European co-operation formed since the War it would have been natural for her to do so. This to my lasting regret the British Government rejected.

On each successive occasion when Britain has attempted to participate, the commitments to be accepted have become greater and the opportunities of shaping the Communities smaller. This continues today. But it is no reason for abandoning the mission. Indeed it is a reason for greater persistence in trying to achieve a successful outcome as soon as possible.

It is interesting, looking back, to examine the underlying reasons why the Labour Government refused to join in the Coal and Steel Community talks. First — and I have no doubt the overall reason, which also influenced Conservative Governments after them — was that they were still thinking of Britain's position in terms of the 1920s and 1930s, indeed in terms of our history during the period of development of the nation state. Whilst the European countries concerned were moving on from the nation state because in their view it was inadequate to meet modern requirements, the British were still thinking in terms of the power which they had previously exercised and which they believed still belonged to them. There is no doubt today that opinion in Britain has changed. The understanding of Britain's comparative power in the modern world is more realistic than it then was. Indeed it may well be that the pendulum has swung too far in the other direction. But there can be no doubt that the belief in interdependence, so skilfully fostered by Mr. Macmillan, and the recognition that Britain can best achieve her purpose in the modern world as a member of a larger grouping has the support today of the majority of British people.

Secondly, the Labour Government was opposed to entering what was and what they believed, as it turned out correctly, was going to continue to be fundamentally a Christian Democratic Europe and not a Socialist Democratic one. Here again the situation has changed. A large section of the Labour movement now seems to hold no objection to joining a Community in which right-wing and Christian Democratic Parties predominate, just as many Socialist parties in Europe have no objection to joining a right-wing-dominated government.

Thirdly, the Labour Government refused to join the discussions on the Schuman Plan because of the fear of the trade union movement that this would interfere with the nationalisation of coal, electricity, gas, and transport, which had already been achieved, and with the nationalisation of steel on which they were then engaged. Once again the Labour Government is busy nationalising steel but they now recognise, especially after the nationalisation by the Italian Government while a member of the Community of its electricity supply industry, that public ownership, provided there is no discrimination, is in no way incompatible with the Treaty of Rome.

In these three respects the conditions in those early days which kept the Labour Government out of Europe have now changed. But I have to confess that the Conservative Government of 1951 onwards disappointed the hopes of its supporters in Europe as well as those at home who expected it to overcome the isolationist tendencies of its Labour predecessor and lead Britain further into Europe. It is true that we formed a very loose association agreement with the Coal and Steel Community, but when in 1957 the time came for the creation of Euratom and the European Economic Community Britain only sent observers to the preliminary stages, who in fact took little part and were soon withdrawn. By this time the remainder of the OEEC countries were dismayed at the prospect of a breakdown in European economic co-operation because of the emergence of a closely knit economic community, and with Britain they tried to negotiate a free trade area with the Community.

Here again we may look at the underlying problems which faced both sides in this venture. As is well known, the negotiations failed. Fundamentally they did so because of a deep-seated belief on the part of the Community that the Community rested on the Treaty of Rome, the main support of which was the common external tariff. To open up the common tariff to accommodate a free trade area with the rest of Europe would, in their view, so weaken the structure of the Community as to undermine its very existence. This was an all important factor in the situation. It was of immense significance for any future negotiations, but it was little understood or appreciated at the time by those outside the Community.

For the British there were three major problems, some of them shared by the other members of the OEEC outside the Community, which led them to believe that full membership of the Community was impracticable. On the other hand, a free trade area of the kind for which the OEEC countries were negotiating would avoid these problems. It would not impinge on British sovereignty except insofar as Britain undertook to abolish her tariffs against the members of the free trade area as a whole, including the Community. It would not interfere with the British system of agricultural support. And as each country could maintain its own external tariff arrangements with the rest of the world, it would enable Britain to continue to admit Commonwealth foodstuffs and raw materials free of duty and to maintain the Commonwealth preferential system.

The negotiations for a free trade area having broken down it was natural that the Seven, Britain and six other OEEC countries — Norway, Sweden and Denmark, Austria, Switzerland, and Portugal — should together form the European Free Trade Association. This was a defensive measure to enable them, having been excluded from the larger Community, to increase trade amongst themselves as well as an attempt to organise a grouping which by becoming attractive to others as a trading organisation, would provide a means of creating in some form or other a wider European market later on. There is no doubt of the success of EFTA as a trading organisation, though the value of this has been greatly underestimated in the United States and elsewhere. However, EFTA has not yet fulfilled its second purpose of being a means of creating a wider European unity. Indeed in some ways its existence has made negotiation with the Community more difficult. Its members have naturally felt an obligation towards each other, hence the British undertaking in 1961 that the arrangements for entry into, or for association with, the Community must all come into operation at the same time. This appeared to the members of the Community to be a formidable undertaking not only from the British point of view but also from their own, involving as it did the future simultaneous assimilation of countries larger in number than their existing membership. In this respect the situation is even more difficult today. During the Brussels negotiations, when the reduction of the internal tariffs of EFTA was only partially achieved, it would have been possible with the agreement of the EFTA countries to arrange a system of gradual adjustment of the EFTA countries' tariffs to the Community and to each other as they became members or associated. Today, now that EFTA is fully established as a free trade area, any difference of time between the joining and association of members with the Community will mean a member putting up its tariffs against its partners while it adjusts itself to the common tariff of the Community. This is not a very happy prospect.

Nevertheless, EFTA has undoubtedly proved of advantage to its members. Moreover, it is apparently the only arrangement possible for the Seven until wider membership of the Community is extended to them. Because of the timing and method of its formation it has never been regarded very favourably either by the Community or by the United States. In particular both have had doubts about the position of the neutral countries. The Community has felt that if countries were going to enjoy the benefits of belonging to an economic community they should also be willing to accept fully the obligations and responsibilities of membership. There has always been a suspicion that the neutral countries were endeavouring to opt out of their responsibilities. The members of the Community who were formerly neutral have been the ones to feel most strongly about this. As for the United States, it has always recognised that the widening of the Community would mean an extension of tariff discrimination against American products. This the United States has been prepared to accept in return for the prospect of a wider and more stable political unity in Europe. If the neutral countries were not prepared to play their part in this then the administration in Washington saw little reason why it should accept further tariff discrimination because of them. This was an understandable position; but there are signs that a wider view is now being taken in Washington. At the same time the neutral countries themselves are beginning to recognise that acceptance of the structure of the Community would not have

such damaging effects on their neutrality as they had previously believed. The main requirement is the ability to
contract out in time of war, and although this may be le-
gally difficult to reconcile with membership of a group like
the Community, in practice it should not be insuperable.

The exception is Austria, which has obligations under the
Peace treaty and the State treaty to which the Soviet Union
is a signatory. The Soviet Union shows every sign of enforc-
ing these obligations. For Austria to become a member of
the Community or closely associated with it is, to the Soviet
Union, not an Austrian problem nor yet an Austro-Soviet
problem. It would in Soviet eyes be equivalent to a reactiva-
tion of the Anschluss between Austria and Germany. It is
therefore, to the Soviet, part of the German problem. Although Austria has now been negotiating on its own with
the Community for three years, no solution has yet been
reached on this aspect of the matter.

EFTA having been safely launched, the British Government decided in the autumn of 1960 to see whether, despite
the obstacles which had previously inhibited it, membership
of the Community would be possible. This was a recognition of the growing success and importance of the Community as well as of the danger of a political division of Western Europe following upon its economic division. I recall
Jean Monnet saying to me in Paris in September 1960: "I
always knew the British would come along to join once they
were convinced the Communities were going to be a success.
And now you have come".

The initiative was taken by Chancellor Adenauer in his
talks with Mr. Macmillan in Bonn in August 1960, a Heads
of Government meeting which is often forgotten. In the
course of the next two and a half years the British Prime
Minister had three meetings with the President of France
on this subject, at Birch Grove, at Champs, and at Ram-

bouillet. All dealt with political matters. The British Prime Minister's meeting with the Italian Prime Minister was forestalled by a week by the sudden break up of the negotiations in January 1963.

After nine months of preliminary discussions with the six member Governments the British Government announced its intention in July 1961 to enter into negotiations under Article 237 of the Treaty of Rome, the Article governing full membership. The other EFTA countries accepted this initiative, some wholeheartedly, some with doubts about the timing, and agreed that each in due course would make its own application, either under Article 237, or under Article 238, dealing with association.

I do not propose to deal with the details of the negotiations here, but I would like to draw certain conclusions from them because of their importance for the future. First, the primary reason why Britain entered into these negotiations was political, political in its widest sense. The British Government saw that any large, prosperous grouping on the mainland was bound to exert political influence, not only over Europe as a whole but also in its relations with the United States and with the developing countries. Although few thought that this influence would be used to the positive disadvantage of Britain, many believed that the best way for Britain to use her own influence in the modern world was as part of such a grouping. Moreover, they were deeply anxious about the possibility, already mentioned, of growing political divisions as the result of two rival economic groupings in Europe. Added to this was the belief that increased economic prosperity as the result of such membership would also enable Britain better to maintain its influence in the Commonwealth, an influence which depended more and more on the supply of capital, aid, and technical know-how.

In Britain a myth has become fashionable that we were concerned only with economic affairs and obsessed with minor details. Nothing could be further from the truth. The main purpose of the negotiations was political. This was made plain at the level of Heads of Governments. It was fully recognised by the members of both the Community and EFTA. In my opening statement in Paris on 10 October 1961 I said: "In saying that we wish to join the EEC, we mean that we desire to become full, wholehearted and active members of the European Community in its widest sense and to go forward with you in the building of a new Europe."

But what is also fundamental is that the three Communities are economic ones, all concerned with different aspects of economic affairs. This priority was deliberately chosen by the architects of the new Europe. They believed that they had first to create an economic basis on which later the political development of Europe could take place. It was therefore natural that although the primary reason for our negotiation was political the negotiation itself was mainly concerned with economic matters. And this will be so with any future negotiation.

But developments in political organisation were not neglected. At the meeting of the Western European Union in London on 18 April 1962 I put forward to the Six the British view of the political organisation of Europe as we would like to see it develop. With it I sketched a preliminary outline of the defence arrangements as its concomitant. These two aspects of European life I shall discuss later.

The second point to remember about the Brussels negotiations is that at that time the Community was at an early stage of its development. For example, when I opened the negotiations in Paris in October 1961 no common agricultural policy was in existence. It is true that general proposals for such a policy had been put forward for discussion but there was a great deal of scepticism as to the extent to which they would be adopted. This had an advantage for us. Had Britain become a member, the rest of the policies of the Community would have been worked out by a membership including ourselves which would take account of our own particular characteristics. But it also had a disadvantage. We were negotiating with a moving escalator. The Six had to meet to agree on every aspect of their own policy before they could negotiate with us as a possible future member. From their point of view there was an inescapable dilemma. Negotiating a solution first among themselves meant a long, often painful, and sometimes in their view premature process, the result of which was later difficult to change in discussion with us. On the other hand to have negotiated straightaway round the table with us on each new item of policy would have left them without any policy for themselves alone had we decided at the end not to join the Community.

The situation is today reversed. The Community has now almost completed its formation. The common tariff will come fully into operation, all internal tariffs will be abolished, a common agricultural policy will be completed, and much of the economic union will have been created by 1 July 1968. This means that Britain can have little influence now on the creation of the fundamental infrastructure of the Community. At the same time, it should be easier to negotiate with members who have already decided what their attitude is on all major aspects of Community life and reached agreement on the details of it. But the very fact that they have reached agreement, sometimes after immense effort, will make it all the more difficult to change the arrangements to accommodate a new member. In this respect therefore any future negotiation will be harder for Britain than the last, because she will have to accept so much more of the structure of the Community as finally settled.

There are some final lessons to be learned from our last negotiations. Two things are impossible to negotiate in an enlarged economic grouping. The first is to maintain the existing patterns of trade untouched. What is the point of entering a Community, its members ask, if the only purpose is to maintain everything exactly as it is? In any case patterns of trade are constantly changing. All over the world the evidence is there to see — the trade in cereals between Canada, the Soviet Union, and China and the immense expansion of trade between Japan and Australia, to mention only two major developments in the last two years.

Secondly, it is impossible to negotiate satisfactorily firm arrangements for a future demand-supply position. This we constantly tried to do in Brussels. I realise now that we were engaged on an almost hopeless quest. Information, estimates, views, and judgements all vary as to the future interaction of individual and group economies on each other when brought together. The practical approach is to recognise the difficulties of negotiating for hypothetical situations and to concentrate on ensuring that satisfactory machinery exists for handling the changes in the balance of economic forces which are bound to be brought about when the Community is enlarged. This particularly applies to agriculture. We were successful on the last occasion in negotiating an agreement for the establishment of a price review for agricultural products in an enlarged Community. This could have been based on a similar national price review where individual countries wished. I believe that whereas it is not possible to convince Foreign Ministers sitting round a table of the future course of supply and demand for any particular agricultural product, nevertheless when developments actually occur they will certainly wish to adjust themselves to them as speedily as possible. It is clear that the machinery for doing so is of the utmost importance.

This brings me to the last, but vital lesson of the negotiations: the urgent necessity of understanding the real nature of the Community. This is not only important in itself. It governs the form of any negotiation which takes place with the Community — hence its relationship to the future.

The European Community has been shaped by its members into the form which best suits them, severally and corporately, though obviously not in all its details individually. Indeed they have made national sacrifices both for the common cause of maintaining the Community and in order to receive individual benefits from it. It is the sort of Community they want and the sort of Community they intend to keep. In their eyes it is a proven success and has come to stay, a view which we would all do well to accept. For too long outside observers have been misled by the superficial political froth covering the activities of the Community without recognising underneath the powerful forces working for economic integration and the methods, sometimes apparently unruly and unorthodox, by which these are handled in the Community itself. The method of work, prolonged argument, highly publicised, often late at night, culminating in a package deal is to say the least unusual. But its justification must be that it has been successful in achieving results.

In the eyes of its members the Community is based on certain fundamental essentials — the Treaty of Rome, the common external tariff, the abolition of all internal tariffs, the common agricultural policy, and the economic union. These are indispensable if the Community is to retain its identity as a Community.

The question therefore posed to any would-be member is a simple one: Is this the sort of Community you like and wish to join? If so, accept us as we are and adapt yourself to become one of us.

Many people have been misled by the use of the vernacular phrase "Common Market". This conjures up a vision of a market place in which everything is open to haggling and bargaining; in which the better haggler or bargainer you are the more likely you are to obtain your way. This is certainly not so. This organisation is much more than a Market. It is a Community. Its members live and work together as such. There are some who believe that to accept the Community in this form is to give away a negotiating card or to risk losing a trick. Exactly the reverse is the case. No negotiation can begin until the Community as a whole is unequivocally accepted. Then and only then will the interests of a would-be new member be considered.

These interests mean predominantly the negotiation of transitional arrangements to change from a country's present position to its future position as a member of the Community. Again, an unreasonable claim provides no strength in a negotiating position. If anything, by conveying an impression of insincerity, it weakens it. Each member of the Community has had to make changes in almost every aspect of its policy. They all know what can be done when the will is there and what can be done under pressure. They know what is a reasonable objective to achieve and to ask others to carry out. One should be realistic in the demands for transitional arrangements.

But more than that, proposals can be negotiated for new machinery for the enlarged Community which can be shown to be in the interests of all its members.

And for the British there are the arrangements for the Commonwealth. These were worked out in great detail almost to the point of completion in Brussels. They are available for any Government which wishes to take advantage of

them, provided the Community is still prepared to adhere
to them.

A considerable amount of negotiation remains to be done
in the case of the accession of any new member. But the
shorter the negotiation the better. Public opinion tires of
protracted discussions on technical subjects, and those who
wish to undermine the negotiations will seize on every difficulty and set-back to do so. Another myth has grown up
that the last negotiations in Brussels were unduly protracted. The negotiations affected the trade, commerce, and
economic activities of some twenty-seven independent
countries together with the British Colonial Empire and the
associated states of the Community. It was the biggest, most
complicated, and most difficult individual negotiation of
modern times. Yet in all they lasted sixteen months, which
compares favourably with the two years taken to negotiate
the Treaty of Rome, itself largely an enabling Treaty.

I have often asked myself whether there was any opportunity of bringing the negotiations more speedily to a conclusion, but I have constantly been forced back on the view
that there was not. The Conference was exhausted when it
finally adjourned at seven o'clock in the morning of Sun-
day, 4 August 1962. There had to be a summer break. After
the meeting of Commonwealth Prime Ministers in the autumn only one or two minor items were brought again before the Conference. It was in no way impeded by them,
and it then got on with the work of dealing with the remaining agricultural and Commonwealth arrangements. And
when Britain and the Six met at the beginning of January
1963 it was well known that it was to be for three weeks, a
week in Brussels, a week back in the capitals, and then a
further week of negotiation in which to arrange a package
deal. I have no doubt that this could have been done.

The negotiation was in fact broken off by the President of

France for political reasons. This he particularly ascribed to the Nassau Agreement, under which Britain obtained Polaris weapons from the United States. At the time I attributed the break up to two different views of the new Europe we were trying to create. I have no doubt that at the time this was true. The problem which has since faced us is whether it is possible to reconcile these two views and if so how, not only in the interests of Europe and the Atlantic Alliance but also in order to secure the success of any future negotiation for British entry.

As to the future, the Community still has some major matters to decide. First, it has to complete the economic union. In this, financial matters, including the question of a common currency, loom large. Final agreement has to be reached on the agricultural financial regulation concerning the disposal of the levies placed on foodstuffs entering the Community. Allied with this is the similar question of the disposal of the proceeds of the customs duties arising from the common tariff imposed at the ports. The logic of the situation undoubtedly is that as this is a common market the dues or levies, no matter where geographically they are imposed, should go to a common pool. This raises immediate problems for those countries where the dues have always been the source of a large part of their revenue. This has to be resolved by 1970.

As for the internal financial arrangements these have become closely interconnected without any formal steps being taken towards a common currency or common financial institutions. The result has been achieved de facto rather than institutionally. In this the Community has been helped by the development of the common agricultural policy with fixed negotiated prices, a common pressure on its members to retain the parity of their currencies which was foreseen by few inside or outside the Community. The fact that its members have now agreed upon the provisions of a value added tax to be applied throughout the Community shows the extent to which they are already developing common fiscal policies. And the results of the regular meetings of the Finance Ministers and governors of the state banks demonstrate how closely they are co-ordinating their financial activities.

There remains also the problem of the implementation of a common commercial policy by the Community. This is due to come into effect by the end of the transitional period in 1970, when it will be handled by the Common Market Commission in Brussels. This means that no individual member will be able to use commercial policy as a means of carrying out its own national foreign policy. One may wonder whether this will be acceptable to President de Gaulle, who has used commercial policy particularly, for example, to further the aims of his foreign policy towards the Eastern Socialist states. I have often felt that the disagreement in the Community in July 1965 between France and the other members was not really over the financial arrangements for the common agricultural policy, for which the French could have obtained a settlement the next day. Nor was it over supra-nationality as such, for the French were already working the system of qualified majority voting and have continued to do so. Indeed, France allowed herself to be outvoted on the 1967 budget for the Community. Rather the French had in mind one particular implication of the provisions for qualified majority voting, namely the decision to implement a common commercial policy.

There are some who believe that the so-called Luxembourg Agreement changed the supra-national provisions of the Treaty of Rome. But the agreement was really an agreement to disagree. All the Six put on record their determination to do their utmost to achieve agreement without a vote on any item of policy which an individual member considered to be of major importance to it. The French insisted on their view that no member could be outvoted on an item which it believed to be of major concern to it. But the Five put on record that if this proved not to be possible the Treaty would prevail. It is not for me to discuss whether or not this has derogated from the Treaty itself. But I remember Jean Monnet saying to me in 1960 when we were discussing the question of sovereignty and supra-nationality that despite the provisions for qualified majority voting in the third stage of the Treaty no major power would be outvoted on a vital matter of national interest because the strain on the life of the Community would be too great and the danger of break-up too obvious for the other members to pursue it.

The problems remaining to be settled are of immense interest to the British as would-be new members. In particular the agricultural financial regulation will affect the British balance of payments. It is difficult to make an exact calculation but it must take account of increased agricultural production at home and an increase in imports from within the Community, accompanied by a corresponding decrease in imports from other outside suppliers. On the question of sovereignty it is in the interests of Britain as of the other members that the Community we join should be an effective one. We therefore have no interest in making it less so. At the same time we acknowledge the practical point Jean Monnet made to me.

This then is my position on future British membership: I firmly believe it to be in the interests of Europe as well as of Britain. Moreover it is in the interests of establishing a better balance in the Atlantic Community. Let us accept the Community as it is, negotiate transitional arrangements and provisions for new machinery where required, and let us implement the arrangements already worked out for the Commonwealth.

But I must add that there are four other important subjects to which agreed solutions have to be found. The first two concern Britain and her relations with the Community. They are the outstanding indebtedness to the International Monetary Fund, some £900 million, the first tranche, some £300 million, to be repaid by the end of 1967 and the remainder by 1970. The second is the long-term balance of payments problem and the operation of the sterling area. Both these items are of rightful concern to the Community because under Article 108 the members accept the obligation of helping each other in times of difficulty. Moreover if a deflationary economy is necessary to achieve the necessary surplus in the balance of payments for the repayment of debt this will obviously make the addition of this new market less attractive to the other members, certainly in the short term.

The other two items are matters on which the Community itself has so far made no progress. They are, thirdly, the development of political institutions and, fourthly, the creation of a defence system for the European Community itself. A solution to these problems is important for the future of the Community, for its impact on other countries, and in particular for a successful negotiation of Britain's membership.

These four points will be discussed more fully in the next two chapters. All of them go to the heart of the matter. They are all aspects of the European attitude which is developing today. They are all connected with attempts to create a European entity to redress the balance in the Atlantic community as a whole. People in Europe today are feeling European. For the young in particular older nationalisms are rapidly disappearing. But with the removal of customs barriers the old frontiers have less and less meaning. With the almost universal use of television everyone can see what is going on in his own continent every day of his life. And the ubiquitous scooter means that not content with seeing the world on the screen the young can go and see for themselves what life has to hold for their generation. Who are their neighbours? From all this stems a European spirit which harks back to the time when Europe was one civilisation, undivided, and which remained until 1939, despite its internecine warfare, the central complex of power politics in the world. Everyone knows that that situation will never recur. But it is not an unworthy ambition to wish one's own continent to have greater influence in the world and to play a responsible part in world affairs.

Never did one man better show an instinctive understanding of any people's spirit than did the late President Kennedy when he said to the assembled multitude in the isolated city "Ich bin Berliner". That summed it up. I saw him a few days afterwards at Mr. Macmillan's home at Birch Grove and I mentioned to him how moved an Englishman had been by his use of such a phrase. I could tell that he felt genuinely committed to those he was then visiting all over Europe and to whom he was so eloquently talking.

It is in a similar spirit that so many today are feeling and thinking not only "I am British or French or German or Italian" but also "I am a European".

II Future Problems of European
Economics and Politics

In my first lecture I discussed the growing pains of the New
Europe and emphasised the emerging desire, not only in the
EEC but in the countries outside it, especially among the
younger generation, to play a part within the Atlantic Alliance and in world affairs more worthy both of Europe's past
history and its future potential. I have no doubt that those
who are building up the Community are constructing their
policies on this basis. But it is also my belief, as I hope I
made clear, that if these ambitions are to be achieved they
can best be done in an enlarged Community of which Britain and other European countries are members. Perhaps I
may briefly illustrate this on the assumption that the Community were to be extended to include either as members or
associates all the EFTA countries. In that case the enlarged
Community market would be some 40 per cent larger in
size of population than the United States. But the United
States gross national product would be 50 per cent greater
and United States output per head twice as large. This
shows the size of the gap between the two sides of the Atlantic. It is true that the growth in output per head over the
five years 1960–1965 was less in the United States than in
the combined European Economic groups, 3.2 per cent as
compared with 3.6 per cent. Nevertheless, if we made an
optimistic assumption that growth in the United States
would consistently rise at 4 per cent and in Europe at 5 per
cent it would still be some forty years before the two econo-

mies would become comparable. In fact, of course, on the average for the past five years and in any likely forecast of growth it would be much longer than forty years. Incidentally, output per head in the EFTA countries is almost 100 dollars a head more than in the Community countries, 1,740 as against 1,650. But on the other hand, growth per head in EFTA over the last five years has been less than in the Community, 3.1 per cent as against 3.9 per cent. The Community is therefore fairly rapidly overtaking the standard of living of the EFTA countries.

Those in Europe who want their continent to forge ahead and to play a larger part in world affairs feel a need to re-dress the balance first of all between the two sides of the At-lantic in four different fields. First in trade and commerce, both industrial and agricultural, of which the proceedings in the Kennedy Round are the current manifestation. Sec-ondly in financial matters in which the current argument about the basis for international monetary transactions is the outward and visible sign. Thirdly the political sphere, in which the long protracted argument over federalism and confederalism is the painful demonstration of a failure to reach any conclusion which would make effective political action possible. And fourthly, in defence, to which the difficulties or as some would say the malaise, in NATO and the North Atlantic Alliance bear witness. It is each of these that I wish to discuss. And to do so not only as to their sub-stance but also in the context of possible British membership in an enlarged Community. In my third lecture I should like to take up the question as to what sort of influence Eu-rope within the Atlantic Alliance can have upon world affairs.

Let me deal now with trade and commerce, agriculture and industry.

The United States Trade Expansion Act was a brilliant

and imaginative attempt to use trade to consolidate the Western world. The fact that President Kennedy initiated it showed his true devotion to the objective of reducing the barriers which divide the Atlantic Community. And the fact that Congress approved it showed how far it had gone to abandon some of those protective measures which were so marked a feature of American policy in earlier years. It was of course originally designed on the hypothesis that Britain and some of the other EFTA countries would become members of the enlarged European Community before the Act became effective. I discussed the draft legislation with President Kennedy's advisers in Washington in 1962, after we had begun the negotiations and before it was published. I welcomed it then as opening up great possibilities for Western co-operation. I still hope that the negotiation will end in success. But we must recognise that there is now little time left.

In any case I do not believe that President Kennedy's original conception of a 50 per cent cut in tariffs across the board, together with a substantial reduction in agricultural protection, can be realised. And for this reason: The countries of the Community, feeling their growing industrial and trading strength, believe that a straight tariff cut across the board, though it has all the advantages of simplicity and was thought at the time to lead to a short negotiation, in fact acts unfairly on the European economies. In addition Europeans believed that it would make any progress towards restoring the balance between the two sides of the Atlantic, already difficult, even more so. In agriculture, in particular, many Europeans feel that for a long period the great producing areas of North America, South America, and Australasia have been the granaries of Europe; whilst in Europe itself agriculture, based on a system of land tenure, which has often led to more and more divided hold-

ings, starved of capital investment and unable to take full
advantage of modern chemicals has not had a chance to re-
spond to the needs of the times. Moreover whereas industrial trade has on the whole tended to balance, trade in agriculture has been a one way trade. The European
Community is therefore now determined to give agriculture
in its own countries a fair crack of the whip and see a better
balance here as well as in trade in industrial goods.

The importance of a successful Kennedy Round to the
two sides of the Atlantic has constantly been emphasised. I
fully endorse it. What has not been so fully appreciated is its
importance for reducing the barriers to intra-European
trade which have grown up between the two economic
groupings of the EEC and EFTA. Until the Common Market is enlarged to take in members of EFTA a successful
Kennedy Round appears to be the only way of reducing the
discrimination between the two groups. It is also important
in reducing the impact on the preferential trade in industrial goods between the older Commonwealth countries,
Canada, Australia, and New Zealand, and Britain should
we become a member of the European Economic Community. For all these reasons I greatly hope that Governments
on both sides of the Atlantic will be able to bring about a
successful outcome to the Kennedy Round of tariff negotiations in the very short time that remains to them.

Let me turn now from trade and commerce to production. As far as both the Common Market and EFTA are
concerned, the situation on marketing is satisfactory, for
each is proceeding to the creation of its own fairly homoge-
neous market. Marketing is all right: but production is not.
We can talk of the common market: we cannot yet talk of a
common production line. On the contrary. So far the removal of trade barriers inside the two groups is tending to
result in greater specialisation within individual countries

and a consequent increase in the size of industrial concerns within — but only within — each country. It is not yet promoting diversification or the development of international undertakings. The rationalisation of the steel industries of Western Europe has, with one exception, been carried out entirely within each country. Perhaps this has been due to a lack of confidence in industry pending the conclusion of the transitional stages of the Community and of EFTA. Or perhaps the truth is that a genuinely European enterprise or firm, one not afraid to cross boundaries — or even the Channel — will only develop when the obstacles that exist in the shape of different tax systems, different company laws, and different domestic laws and practices are removed. In the case of the Community this will be when the economic union is completed. In the case of EFTA its convention makes no provision for integration of this kind.

The failure to use the liberalisation of trade to establish more international industrial enterprises is extremely disappointing. It means that industrialists in the countries of the Six still view with some misgiving the widening of their own economic scope within the Community. And some still tend to view the admission of a new member as the advent of a competitor instead of as an opportunity for industrial growth on an international level. This is economic myopia. For failure to look to the market as a whole beyond their own national boundaries is imposing limitations on growth such as to invite the very consequences — takeovers from abroad — which they are seeking to resist. Rationalisation, specialisation, economics of scale — all these may enable European industries to market probably all that they can produce. But they do nothing to alleviate the constraints increasingly imposed on them by shortage of capital for the purposes of research and development, constraints that effectively hinder the necessary expansion of European industries.

What then can be done to encourage European industry to become more international in its outlook and attitudes? One answer might be to create a new type of Eurocompany with special status and subject to special laws and conditions — particularly in the field of taxation — different from those applied to national companies in any individual European country. But I doubt whether economic union within the EEC is sufficiently advanced at this stage to embark on the complex task of negotiating the conditions for such a Eurocompany status with any hope of immediate success. The problem of doing this for Western Europe as a whole is of course far greater. We have already tried for four years to secure agreement on common industrial measurements and standards and a common convention for patents but with scant success.

The alternative is the ad hoc development of specific co-operative ventures between industries in the different European countries. There already exist plenty of examples of such arrangements in the field of oil marketing, motor car assembly, photographic material, to name but a few. But the major examples in this field are provided by the joint development of vast new enterprises, either directly or indirectly encouraged by the State, the scale of which makes it impossible for the industry of one European nation to develop it by itself. The Concord supersonic airliner is the outstanding example of this. Another is the Anglo-Belgian co-operation in the development of certain types of atomic reactors. The areas in which this kind of co-operation can take place are bound to be limited. Moreover, they will be the subject of political choice. It is therefore worth considering which fields of co-operation should be selected and what kind of technological gain can be derived from such ventures.

There has recently been a great deal of publicity for the proposal to form a new European technological community. I doubt whether, as an institutional proposal, this is acceptable to the Six at a time when the executives of the three existing communities are about to be fused, to be followed later by the fusion of the three communities themselves. But for me another aspect also detracts from its value. Such a community would deal with governmental technology and its projects. I believe that the real breakthrough in depth in European technology has to come within private industry itself through the activities of larger European firms such as I have been describing.

For Europe merely to duplicate the efforts of the United States in technology would be a waste of time and energy. A secondhand technology is bad enough, but to waste resources on rediscovery is even worse. And yet the temptations to go in for precisely this duplication are strong. We must recognise that in Europe there is bound to be a reaction against the way in which control of these technologically advanced industries is increasingly passing into American hands. This is not an expression of anti-Americanism: it is the not unnatural desire to retain control over the achievements brought about by one's own skill and brain power.

It is also the by-product of the fact that great American firms can deploy resources for research and development on a scale unmatched by individual industries in individual European countries. What an American firm can do a whole European industry is very often incapable of matching. Europeans are losing out in the very areas, such as computers, in which they should be co-operating.

Another case in point is the aircraft industry. A national

airline has strong grounds for standardising its fleet. Economies in spares, servicing, and the training of both ground
and air crews predisposes them to obtain aircraft of every
range and type from the same manufacturer. Most national
airlines, even quite small ones, fly a whole range of aircraft.
But no single European country has the resources to develop and produce, competitively, the full range that its airline is likely to require.

It is a sobering thought, for example, that while the value
last year of the British aircraft industry's output was more
than one and a half billion dollars, its home sales of civil
aircraft amounted to little more than 100 million dollars.
And that 62 per cent of its income was derived from Government procurements and aid towards research and development. But if the French, German, and British aircraft industries got together they could, I am quite certain, produce
the range of aircraft required by each of their national airlines. Initially, perhaps, this might involve some duplication
of American research, though the present advanced state of
British aircraft technology suggests that the duplication
would be minimal. It is not after all the basic ideas that we
in Britain and Europe lack; it is the ability to put them into
practice. Once such a range of European aircraft is produced, development in Europe will at least keep pace with
that in America, and there would be co-operation between
the two industries for the aircraft markets of the world.

The example of the aircraft industry illustrates the paradox of research and development resources in Europe. Nationally, no single country has sufficient resources to compete successfully with the giant American companies in the
technologically advanced industries. And the inability to
compete commercially means that the finance for research
and development cannot be afforded. If Britain were spending on research and development the same proportion of

her expenditure on capital goods that the United States is spending, she would have to increase her output on research by 50 per cent. It has been estimated that for every 1,000 dollars spent on research both public and private in America, only 100 dollars is spent in Britain, 75 dollars in France, and a mere 50 dollars in Germany. Again the gap between the two sides of the Atlantic is illustrated. It is natural that Americans should want to invest the knowledge gained from this research into a profitable expansion of their industries, and they are in a position to do so. But they are inhibited by their antitrust laws from expanding through mergers and takeovers at home. So they naturally look abroad, particularly to Europe, for an outlet for their accumulation of brain capital.

For Europe this has serious consequences. There is nothing wrong with importing technology. But we should beware of the dangers that this implies. European industry cannot afford to become so dependent on its imported technology as to allow its own brains to become flaccid and dispirited. Already, resources in Europe particularly of skilled manpower are underemployed because the facilities for research and development are inadequate. This is one of the main causes of the brain drain from Europe to the United States. The drain from Britain and Germany is severe. In 1965 more than five hundred engineers emigrated from Britain to America, and three hundred from Germany. And this trend is continuing. M. Robert Marjolin, Vice President of the Common Market Commission, told the Assembly in Strasbourg last October: "If the Six European Community countries remain, as they probably have done for a generation, the world's main importers of discoveries, and its main exporters of brains, they will be condemning themselves to a cumulative under-development which will soon make their decline irrevocable." But if the drain on the resources of brain power is damaging to Britain, Germany, and to a lesser extent France, what does it do to countries like Switzerland, Norway, the Netherlands, and Greece, where more than twenty out of every hundred engineers graduating from their universities find their way across the Atlantic?

This then is the result of inadequate resources in individual industries in individual European countries. There are, of course, some projects which do not lack money for development because they are obviously of great commercial value. In a very short time it was possible to finance the exploration of the North Sea gas fields to the tune of at least 300 million dollars, for the return on this kind of development is very likely to be worthwhile. There are, however, some projects which may never be worthwhile to private industry from a commercial point of view. Expenditure on space research clearly falls into this category. I am not suggesting for a moment that Europe should or could compete in this field with a programme for landing on the moon. But there probably is a case for the European Launcher Development Organisation since a European communications satellite programme makes sense. While noncommercial expenditure on research and development must be a matter of political choice, it will tend to be concentrated on those areas which can be sold to the taxpayer — glamorous projects like the launcher programme and necessary projects like defence. If it is true that these are the only areas in which the taxpayer can be persuaded to subsidise research and development, expenditure which is not commercially justified, we must ask ourselves whether the external returns or fall-out from such programmes provide a sufficient additional justification for them.

There is no doubt that expenditure on space research gives rise to extremely valuable fall-out. The question is rather whether this fall-out, or "spin-off" as it is known over here, more than compensates for the cost of deploying high-grade resources on a commercially nonviable project rather than in other ways. It is practically an impossibility to calculate the value of the fall-out or, for that matter, the cost of lost opportunities to use resources in other directions. But while academics, for instance, could let the matter rest there, politicians cannot. Decisions have to be made, either consciously or by default, and so we must use whatever evidence we can as a basis for such decisions.

I understand that the United States in 1966 spent about 15 billion dollars on space research. It is not a programme to be judged on economic or commercial considerations, but it has produced a considerable spin-off of real commercial value. Fifteen billion dollars is a lot of money to spend in anyone's language. It may be possible to gain some comprehension of the real magnitude of the United States contribution to space developments as well as to understand the present impossibility of even the whole of Europe thinking in these terms if we try to get some idea of what the impact of an alternative use for such resources would have been. Suppose it had been applied to private investment. An extra 15 billion dollars would probably increase private investment in the United States by some 15 per cent and raise the share of the American gross national product going to private investment from $14\frac{1}{2}$ per cent to over $16\frac{1}{2}$ per cent.

Economists sometimes relate a country's growth rate to the share of output it devotes to investment. On the basis of such calculations, an extra 15 per cent on private investment in the United States might increase the growth of capacity by 10 per cent or more. This gives some measure of what may be termed "the opportunity cost" of the space research programme. It does give some indication of the problem which faces Europe in giving for projects of this size.

It is impossible in practice, and in theory, to measure the benefits of technological advance. Inventions in the past have not merely changed growth rates, but have completely revolutionised our way of life. A balance must be struck however between expenditure on basic research and expenditure exploiting the results of such research. It is often supposed that for every one dollar spent on basic research, ten dollars are needed for development, and a hundred dollars are needed at the production stage. If some such relationship exists, an unbalanced effort can lead to a flow of new ideas outstripping resources available for their exploitation. It is sometimes argued with a great deal of truth that we in Britain concentrate too much of our resources on basic research and too little on commercial development. The swing-wing aircraft is but one example. The same may well be true of Europe as a whole.

I conclude therefore that the Governments of the European Community should be trying to give as powerful a fillip as they can to developments through international co-operation in those fields that hold a prospect of commercially viable end-products. Prestige projects will need careful scrutiny. Resources should not be diverted from the commercially viable programmes without it being quite clear what is to be gained from them. I would like to see the inventiveness of the Old World stretching out to new horizons, using traditional skills and know-how to push back the frontiers of knowledge rather than to consolidate those that exist. And there are plenty of areas where it would be highly worthwhile for the European nations to co-operate on research and development and to invest resources in commercial exploitation.

But how great are the resources that can be devoted to such projects? As far as Britain is concerned the inhibiting factor, which is likely to be of overriding importance for some time to come, is that the level of domestic activity is conditioned by the requirements of the external balance of payments. This is one way in which the problem of sterling impinges on the development of European co-operation. But the other, as I have pointed out, is that the position of sterling as a reserve currency is one of the four issues to which in my view solutions must be found before Britain can achieve membership of the Community. Members of the European Economic Community undertake in effect to hold their exchange rates constant in terms of each other's currency. If Britain were to become a member of the Community, such an undertaking must involve the European countries in a commitment to support directly or indirectly the parity of sterling. That is why the position must be quite clear to the member countries before they can consider Britain's application.

But the sterling problem probably cannot be solved in a European context in isolation from the wider world payments problem, because in part the sterling problem arises from its international role. There seems to be considerable confusion about the exact interconnection between these problems. The first thing to be noticed is that sterling's international role has two distinct elements, that of a reserve currency and that of a trading currency. I wish to deal with them separately.

Sterling's role as a reserve currency, by and large, is part of the overall international liquidity problem. It is not, in fact, a particular burden for the United Kingdom. The contribution of sterling to official international reserves has in fact declined over the past ten years and official holders have shown distinct forebearance during sterling crises and have not added to the United Kingdom's problems by withdrawing funds when sterling has been under pressure. Official sterling holdings may of course be run down when sterling area countries are themselves running payments deficits. However, this does not of itself represent a threat to sterling providing Britain's own balance of payments is itself healthy and the City of London can fulfil its functions of attracting capital from other sources. There are of course vital differences of approach to economic policy between the Government and the Opposition in Britain today. But it is true to say that both major Parties are agreed on the need to build up a surplus on the balance of payments, though the methods to be used by each Party vary.

Since the War Britain has been caught in a vicious circle as far as her balance of payments are concerned. The level of the reserves has proved on occasion to be insufficient to sustain the demand for imports associated with rapid expansion of the economy. This has meant that it has not been possible to keep unit costs at a level which would have enabled exports to expand fast enough to cover the rapid rise in imports required for the growth. When this situation arose under the Conservative Government we found it necessary to deal with the problem by a sharp dose of deflation. This medicine was effective, usually in a comparatively short time, though it naturally had its impact on the amount of growth achieved over this period. In 1963 and 1964 when Mr. Maudling was at the Exchequer and I was at the Board of Trade we were trying to break through this vicious circle. We believed that it was possible to do this, so long as we maintained the confidence of the rest of the world in sterling, which we were able to do right up to the general election of 1964.

The position remains that fundamentally the most important task facing Britain today is to ensure that not only in the short term but in the long term her balance of payments is in surplus. The balance of payments is improving today, and this improvement must be maintained. I do not believe that changes in the exchange rates are the answer to our problems. I do not believe they are necessary on the basis of comparative price levels in export markets. Nor do I believe that any change in rates which would be acceptable to other countries without their changing their own rates would be sufficient to jack up British exports to an appreciable degree which could be sustained on a long-term basis. Indeed there is a danger that people will immediately accept a change in the exchange rate as being the sole measure needed to deal with the situation when in fact more fundamental changes are required in the economy. And I therefore reject the change in the exchange rate as being in any way a solution to our problems.

I am now dealing with domestic matters into which I do not wish to go in any great detail. But my Party has put forward specific proposals for bringing about fundamental structural changes in our economic life which would of course benefit the balance of payments. A change from the support price system for British agriculture to the levy import system, a change in the balance of taxation to provide incentives both to individuals and companies, the reform of trade union legislation, the recasting of the social services, a massive increase in training for management and skilled labour, and a better use of existing resources both of labour and capital are part of this programme.

Where then does the international liquidity problem come into all this? It impinges on the problem by setting the climate in which these fundamental changes have to be made to the British economy. Some European countries, not only France, have criticised Britain and the United States, the countries running the world's two reserve currencies, for our continuing balance of payments deficits. This they have done on the basis that the Europeans have had to support their reserve currencies which meant indirectly supporting economic and sometimes political policies of which they did not approve but which were the cause of the deficits. But if America and Britain do in fact bring their balance of payments into equilibrium the growth in world liquidity will moderate. Over the past decade world reserves have declined in proportion to world trade from about 60 per cent to 40 per cent. Within the overall picture, the American deficit and loss of gold has meant that reserves for all other countries have in fact risen as rapidly as trade. Since in the mid-1950s international reserves were by any standards unduly concentrated in the United States, the redistribution of reserves has counteracted the effects of their slow growth elsewhere so that the symptoms of a world liquidity shortage have been held in abeyance. It seems highly unlikely that when Britain and America are no longer in payments deficit other countries will be willing to see their reserves decline, either in total or in relation to their trade. This is the real problem of international liquidity. Countries whose payments balance move into deficit when the reserve countries earn a surplus will probably take defensive action, by deflating or possibly, since it is an option open to them, by changing the parity value of their currencies. The weight of adjustment in the scramble for liquidity will then be thrown back upon the reserve currency countries, who at present have no option but to meet it by deflation. Thus we would again be in a downwards spiral; hence the need for a solution to the problem of world liquidity. Moreover I would suggest that the pace of the negotiations on the international liquidity front desperately needs to be speeded up.

I wish now to deal with the second aspect of sterling I mentioned: its use as a trading currency. The trading use of sterling takes two forms: it is used as the unit of account in which international transactions are denominated, and it is used as a medium of exchange between countries. So long as the facilities offered by London for transferring funds, for raising credit to finance trade, and for employing funds at short notice are unmatched elsewhere, sterling will be used as a medium of exchange. Traders all over the world will continue to invoice their trade in sterling. And banks all over the world will hold sterling balances to facilitate settlements. You cannot issue a world order telling them not to do so.

Speculation against sterling, at times of crises, predominantly takes the form of leads and lags in trade payments, the withdrawal of commercially held sterling balances, and sterling borrowing. But given a sound correction of our underlying payments deficit, speculative flights from sterling would probably be short-lived and not carry the dangers at present associated with such movements. Hence the fundamental importance of economic policies which would get the balance of payments in surplus. It is reasonable in these conditions to expect the European countries to continue to support sterling against such movements as they are already doing through Basle-type assistance.

I do not believe there is any insuperable problem from a purely British point of view on the international financial side to Britain joining Europe, though there is a need for the international liquidity problem to be dealt with in the context of getting the British economy right and therefore of British membership in the Common Market. This side of the question needs to be settled satisfactorily at an early stage.

I wish now to turn to the question of the political organisation of the Community in which so little progress has so far been made. As I have already emphasised, if Europe wants to make itself effective in world affairs it must find a way of co-ordinating the individual positions of its members much more closely, to say the least. This applies just as

much to the Community alone. It is true that the Bonn
Declaration of July 1961 envisaged much closer co-operation between the countries of the Six in political and defence matters. The Fouchet Committee was set up and produced its plan for a loose organisation for consultation
between the member countries. This however was never im-
plemented. In its final form the Fouchet Plan had the ap-
proval of the President of France, who indeed was credited
with having rewritten a considerable part of it himself. It
also had the support of a number of the other members of
the Six as a first step towards the full political system they
wanted to create. It was unacceptable to the Netherlands,
who have always adhered to the concept of a federal organisation in Europe. The Netherlands Government did however indicate that it was prepared to adopt the Fouchet
Plan provided that Britain was a member of the Community. In those circumstances it said it would have confidence
in the political balance which would then exist within the
enlarged community. This argument led to a particular
form of "dialogue des sourds" between the Governments of
France and the Netherlands, in which neither side pre-
vailed. The French accused the Dutch of undermining the
possibility of political co-operation by insisting on federalism. The Dutch accused the French of preventing the possibility of working the Fouchet Plan by keeping out the British. The French replied by questioning the attitude of the
Dutch in wanting to bring in the British, who were not committed to federalism. This is one of the reasons why there
has been no progress in political co-operation in Europe.

For our part during the negotiations we said at the Western European Union Conference in London in April 1962
that we were fully prepared to take our part in the discussions on the Fouchet Plan should we be invited to do so. We
recognised that we had no rights in the matter because we

were not yet members of the Community; but as we were negotiating for membership we felt it right to offer our participation. This would have enabled the Dutch to accept the Fouchet proposals and allowed a balanced political growth of the Community to develop at the same time as the economic measures were coming into effect and the negotiations were continuing. But this British offer was interpreted in some quarters as being an attempt to slow up the political development of the Community. Such was certainly not the intention. The offer was made in good faith and we hoped it would be accepted. However, the British position was in any case difficult. If we had not made the offer we could well have been accused of showing no interest in the political development of the Community, and this could have been held against us. But making the offer exposed us to the attack of interfering in the affairs of a group of which we were not a member. The same position still applies today.

As far as the general institutions of the Community are concerned I believe that pressure of events will force them to move more and more towards some democratic control of the Council of Ministers and the Commission. Indeed I believe that if the British were to become members of the Community they might well take the lead in this, despite their previous anxieties about supra-nationality, not only because of their long traditions of Parliamentary control of the executive but also because of the practical needs of the hour. It was that great world statesman Sir Robert Menzies who constantly emphasised that a customs union cannot stand still and has no alternative but to go forward to democratic control or to go back to national systems. There is a great element of truth in this.

The practical reasons for more democratic control are these: When a Minister reports a decision of the Council of

Ministers to his own Parliament he may at times have to say that the policy is a compromise one for which he himself has made sacrifices as well as gaining benefits. Or he may have to announce that the decision is the result of a majority vote, in which his own proposals were outvoted. In these cases his Parliamentarians will become anxious to express their views not only to their own Minister but to the body responsible as a whole for the decision which has been taken. The European Parliament at Strasbourg can hardly yet be described as a body of this kind. But as the Community becomes more and more closely integrated I believe there will be increasing demand for such an organisation and the pressure for it to be effective will mount.

This is not to say that there must be direct elections across the whole of Europe for such a Parliament, much as some countries, in particular the Italians, would like it. It should be possible to achieve results, certainly in the first instance, by indirect election. After all the United States Senate, probably the most powerful individual Parliamentary body the world has ever seen, built up its power and influence for the first hundred or so years of its life on the basis of indirect election. The Europeans could well take heart and encouragement from this.

But still the argument about a federal or a confederal Europe persists. It seems to me to be at best a sterile debate and at worst a positive hindrance to European progress, especially when holding one or the other view is held to be the real touchstone of a true European. Dr. von Brentano, a true European if ever there was one and a most distinguished Foreign Minister of the Federal German Republic once said to me that when he first took part in the developments in Europe he thought that Ministers should call together the constitutional lawyers and instruct them to produce a blueprint for the constitution of the new Europe.

"But now" he said to me "I realise there is no possibility of this happening. What is more I do not believe any longer that it is desirable. Here we are not dealing with some new country taking unto itself a constitution for the first time. We are dealing with ancient nation states with long traditions, hopes, aspirations and deep-rooted prejudices. What I believe is now happening" he went on "is that the more closely we work together in economic affairs so gradually will we create the other institutions which are required by a wider European economic unity. And then every ten years I shall invite the constitutional lawyers to tell us which position we have reached — whether it is confederal or federal or something in between".

"That" I replied, "is a typically pragmatic, British approach and very acceptable to us. The only thing is," I added, "that by the time the constitutional historians have decided where we have got to we shall have got to somewhere else".

In effect there are two different ways of measuring political development. One can think in terms of institutions and say that a European political community comes into being only when there is a European executive, a European legislature, and a European judiciary. From what I have already said you will realise that in my view we shall take a long time to reach this point. But it is equally sound to define a political community in terms of the content of its decisions; that is, to say that a European political community comes into being when most of the decisions which are the stuff of political debate in any country are taken on a community basis. By that definition the EEC, using the established institutions of the Council of Ministers and the Commission, is already moving steadily towards a political community. If it succeeds in becoming an economic union in 1970 then a new range of subjects which are the essence

of politics, for example the form of taxation or the level of
social security, will be added to those already taken by the
Community as a whole. Much domestic legislation will of
course remain to individual countries and Parliaments.

There is an important gap, and that is foreign policy.
When fresh proposals are made in the political field, for
example, the Italian proposal for a summit meeting of the
EEC in Rome in April 1967, they are primarily aimed at
filling this gap. The foreign policies of the Six are not
aligned, and there is no machinery at present for bringing
them into line. It is paradoxical that useful discussions on
policy towards say the Soviet Union are held inside NATO,
and also within the Western European Union (Six plus
Britain), but not within the EEC itself. There is no reason of
principle why such discussions should not take place regu-
larly within the EEC as suggested in the Fouchet Plan. The
difficulty is not that the French object in principle to meeting to align foreign policies. The French are reluctant because they believe that the gap between French foreign policy and the foreign policies of the Five, and even more of
Britain, is in practice so wide that alignment is impossible.
That is why the French refused to go to the last meeting of
this kind to which the Italians invited them in Venice in
1965.

But foreign policy must shift with events, and there is no
reason to suppose that a gap which seems too wide to bridge
today will always remain so, particularly if there is a will to
reduce it. There have been persistent efforts by the Five to
provide a framework of regular meetings in which foreign
policy can be aligned, and one day, if not at once then at
some later attempt, I believe they will succeed.

III Europe and the Wider World

The influence of the new Europe on world security falls, I think, naturally into two parts: first what Western Europe can accomplish or help others to accomplish in the world outside Europe: and secondly what Western Europe can do to overcome the division of Europe between East and West.

For centuries the problem of world security was essentially a European problem. The concept of the balance of power, together with an intricate network of alliances, was the dominating factor in the foreign policies of the great European states. Then, during the latter part of the nineteenth century and the first decades of the present century, there came into being for the first time a structure of world security. This was based on the dominance of the European colonial powers in Asia and in Africa, and by the United States in the Pacific and in Latin America. It was a haphazard system, unorganised, possibly unjust, certainly undemocratic, but generally effective.

That structure of security has now largely collapsed through two World Wars. It cannot be said unfortunately that the advent of the nuclear deterrent has made some structure of security unnecessary. While there is a sufficient balance of nuclear weapons in the world to make total war between great powers less likely, the balance of terror does nothing to abolish smaller wars. Indeed, it probably makes smaller disorders more likely by the fact that the freedom of action by the great powers has become more limited. The burden of maintaining world security in these circum-

stances has moved entirely away from Europe. It is on the
United States that the main burden has fallen.

The United States has found itself forced to extend to
Asia and to some extent Africa the responsibilities which by
tradition it exercised in Latin America and the Pacific
alone. In doing so it has poured out vast sums of money. It
has had to fight two costly wars in distant countries of Asia,
with which it was not in the past closely concerned, for ob-
jectives which were not clear-cut. It has found itself guaran-
teeing Governments over whose internal and external policies it has had little control. This, as Britain discovered in
the Middle East and elsewhere, is far more frustrating and
difficult than to exercise direct colonial power. It has found
that American motives in taking up these new responsibilities have been challenged, not only by the enemies of the
United States, but on occasions by some of its friends.

In 1945 the United Nations was designed to discharge
just those responsibilities for world security which have
since in large part fallen on the United States. After twenty
years it is possible to see fairly clearly what kind of problems
the UN is good at tackling and what kind of problems it
does much better to leave alone. Those who disregard this
experience and urge Governments to throw every political
problem into the lap of the UN as if the organisation had
magical powers do it no service at all. It is still reasonable to
hope that the UN will serve as the foundation for an eventual world order; it is not reasonable to treat it as if it were
already a world government.

In what kind of situation can the UN sensibly be asked to
help? I am talking here of political problems, not of the
efforts of the UN and its specialised agencies in the economic and social fields. The UN is best regarded as an additional instrument of diplomacy, to be used when the traditional instruments are not working properly and when

there is a reasonable chance of success. This was essentially the approach of Dag Hammarskjold.

There are I suggest two conditions which normally have to be satisfied before the UN can act in a situation with a reasonable hope of success. First, there should not be a *direct* confrontation of the great powers; the UN cannot hope to impose its will on these. Second, the problem should not arouse the strong emotions of the majority of the UN members, since these emotions prevent the UN from acting as a conciliator.

One can think of several examples where these two conditions have been satisfied and where, as a result, the UN has been able to act as a peace-keeper in a way which would not have been possible for individual powers or groups of powers. In Palestine for example the UN Truce Supervisory Organisation and the UN Emergency Force patrol the frontiers between Israel and her Arab neighbours. In Cyprus another UN force with a British element prevents the Greek and Turkish communities from slaughtering each other. In Kashmir UN observers still watch the cease-fire line. These are all examples of disputes between medium-sized or small powers which have brought those powers to war or to the brink of war. In none of these disputes are the emotions of the majority of UN members closely involved. As a result the UN has been able to act as a conciliator, and to introduce a local UN presence which has helped to damp down the conflict.

But in none of these cases has a final solution to the dispute been found. It is in situations of this kind that the UN should be encouraged to play a more active diplomatic role. The Secretary-General and the Secretariat are still better placed than anyone else to take an initiative to settle the Arab-Israeli dispute, which every two or three years threatens to destroy the stability of the Middle East. They are well placed to attempt to reconcile the two communities in Cyprus. They have an opportunity now in Arabia itself following the British Government's invitation to the General Assembly to send a mission to South Arabia, though the precedent of the UN effort in the Yemen is not encouraging. The Secretary-General should be made to feel that he has the support of the major powers in carrying out more actively the mandates already entrusted to him and in looking for new opportunities for conciliation. If the UN is encouraged in these directions it still has a chance of growing on its own achievements until it is really, in the words of the Charter, "a centre for harmonising the actions of nations in the attainment of . . . common ends".

Western Europe by reason of its prosperity ought to make a growing contribution to another aspect, to the economic underpinning which we all now accept as a condition of world stability. The European contribution, like the American, ought to be a considered mix of different economic weapons. More than that, my experience of leading the British Delegation at the United Nations Conference on Trade and Development in 1964 has convinced me that the problems of the developing countries, in particular the ever-widening gap in the standard of living between them and the Western industrialised world, can be met only by a combined effort between the three major groups with the capability of making it, namely the United States, Britain, and the European Economic Community. If this effort is to be made, then traditional habits of thought will have to change. Britain will have to give up its traditional opposition to world commodity agreements at anything other than the lowest possible price. The Community, led by France, may have to be prepared to grant more financial assistance and extend its attitude towards preferential markets to include more developing countries. The United States may have to give up its resistance to preferences of all kinds to the extent of granting limited preference for specific periods to the developing countries. If all three groups (or two groups if Britain were a member of the Community) could agree each to change its traditional attitude in those directions, each being prepared to make a proportional contribution in a way in which they have not hitherto done, I believe a major step forward could be taken towards helping the developing countries. Moreover I am sure this is in the interest of the Western World as a whole. Nothing is more important than to prevent East/West tension being replaced by tension over what Sir Alec Douglas-Home termed when he was Prime Minister "the North/South Gap".

I also believe it right to get away in this field from the concept of spheres of influence. A million British pounds or French francs spent teaching and training Latin Americans may sometimes achieve more than the equivalent sums in US dollars, simply because the American teacher comes to be taken for granted or even resented in an area where the American presence is overfamiliar. The reverse is probably true in Africa, where the American teacher with new methods and new textbooks may call into being fresh vigour and enthusiasm. I am in favour of co-ordinating aid, but not if this is a euphemism for encouraging each country simply to carry on helping by traditional methods the countries in which it has long had interests.

I want now to mention two matters of which little is said in this country and which are often dismissed by the hard-headed in Britain today as myths without practical importance. I mean the Commonwealth and the so-called special relationship between Britain and the United States.

In the Commonwealth there has been a development over the last year or so which has not yet been fully recognised. It needs a little historical explanation. You will know that the Commonwealth evolved between the two Wars as a grouping of Britain, her large colonial empire, and the four independent White Dominions, which, while enjoying complete sovereignty continued to have the same head of state as Britain, that is the Sovereign. There were of course all kinds of other links, notably a common language, the same basis of common law, a common experience of the same form of administration, the same sort of professional and other associations, and numerous personal and family ties. In addition there has always been a constant flow of information and a continuous process of consultation between all parts of the Commonwealth and Empire. I believe that if Britain becomes part of the EEC all this in its modern form will remain. After the 1932 Ottawa Agreements, these links were strengthened by a mutual exchange of trade preferences. These have since been reduced as the result of post-War multilateral trading agreements.

On the political side the main concern of the old Dominion Governments, particularly the Canadian, was in those days to make sure there was no link with Britain which would prevent them from following their own policies as sovereign states. In practice, as they showed in 1939, all four Dominions were ready to make Britain's quarrel their own, but they did not want to be bound in advance to do so. Over the last twenty years the Commonwealth has been enormously enlarged to include the great majority of territories which have gained their independence from British rule. The constitutional connection has been diluted in that most of these countries now have their own heads of state, while recognising the Queen by the new title of Head of the Commonwealth. The newcomers from Asia, Africa, and the Caribbean entered the Commonwealth because they were satisfied from its past working that membership would not mean any restraint on the full sovereign freedom which they had just achieved.

The periodical meetings of the Commonwealth Prime Ministers in London used to be organised by the British Government, which took great care that they should be run as discussions between equals and that the susceptibilities of individual members as to their own sovereignty should be fully respected. Immense trouble was taken, for example, to avoid any discussion in the Conference of the Kashmir dispute between India and Pakistan, two member countries. A break in this tradition came when South Africa withdrew from the Commonwealth after realising that her domestic policies were so repugnant to its members that it would be impossible for her to remain. But recently there have been two new linked developments. A Commonwealth Secretariat has been set up in London to make arrangements for Commonwealth meetings and to organise the exchanges of information and other activities which were formerly the responsibility of the Cabinet Office and the Commonwealth Relations Office, British Government Departments. In January and again in September last year the Commonwealth Prime Ministers held detailed discussions of the Rhodesian question in which strong pressure was put on the British Government. In September the communique emerging from the meeting contained definite undertakings by the British Prime Minister as to how his Government would handle the Rhodesia problem, including a time limit for negotiations with the Rhodesian regime, and an undertaking to propose mandatory sanctions in the Security Council if negotiations failed. The British Government defended these undertakings with the argument that if they had not been given one or more member states would have left the Commonwealth.

I am not concerned here with the merits of the undertakings given over Rhodesia or of the policy pursued. The interesting point is that the Commonwealth seems to have drifted into a position where one member, and one member alone, is expected to submit its policies for examination of a kind which other members would not dream of accepting, and that one member is Britain. The anxieties expressed by the Dominion Governments when the Commonwealth was evolving have been stood on their head; it is now the British Government which must approach Commonwealth Conferences with the fear that its freedom of action will be impaired. Many people in Britain might have been prepared in the past to accept a Commonwealth in which there was a genuine pooling of sovereignty by all, though that vision never became a reality. But I doubt whether the present one-sided state of affairs can continue and I believe the members of the Commonwealth should return to their previous long-established practice at Prime Ministers' meetings of not discussing matters which affect each other's sovereignty. This would be even more necessary with Britain as a member of the Community, though I believe the consultation which normally goes on between Britain and the Commonwealth would become even more valuable. Moreover Britain's membership of the EEC would carry with it in the case of all the developing countries many favourable opportunities of larger markets and increased aid and technical assistance.

It is too often assumed that unless the Commonwealth has a direct and clear political role it can have no profitable existence. I do not believe that is so. In fact the Commonwealth can be expected to continue to flourish as a means of helping forward the innumerable contacts between groups and individuals I have described as well as in trade and aid.

Something of the same argument applies to the so-called special relationship between Britain and the United States. This may well be a strange phrase even in New England. To hear some people talk in Europe one would think that the world is in fact run by the British Prime Minister and the President of the United States meeting daily in conclave in a command post on some island in the middle of the Atlantic. This belief stems of course partly from the wartime partnership of Churchill and Roosevelt and partly from the instinct, which is obviously sound, that Britain and the United States will always have much in common, the same basis of language, law, and custom and innumerable professional and personal ties. It is also true that in day-to-day matters of government there is an instinctive tendency among some British officials when assessing foreign reactions to a particular situation to ask first and foremost what the United States will think and how it will react. In military matters this tendency is particularly noticeable and natural because of the history of the Anglo-American nuclear partnership and the present British reliance on American military equipment. But in government one quickly learns that as one symptom of the shift of power in the modern world the instinct is no longer so strong in Washington. As Britain becomes more closely involved in Europe the instincts of officials will no doubt turn more to Paris, Bonn, or Rome, though I must also add sometimes there has been little sign of this.

One side effect of greater unity in Europe and greater European weight in world affairs might be a reapprisal in Washington of the technique of taking decisions on matters of interest to America's allies. The present process of semi-public debate between different government agencies culminating in a compromise reached or imposed at the last minute often leaves very little room for genuine consultation with friends and allies.

I have dealt with the Anglo-American partnership. What are the prospects for Atlantic partnership? You will remember the speech of President Kennedy at Philadelphia in

1962. "The United States," he said, "will be ready for a Declaration of Interdependence — that we will be prepared to discuss with a united Europe the ways and means of forming a concrete Atlantic partnership, a mutually beneficial partnership between the new union now emerging in Europe and the old American Union founded here a century and three-quarters ago". I think it would be fair to say that this idea of Atlantic partnership corresponds to the eventual hope of the great majority of the peoples of Europe and the United States. But President Kennedy saw that only a united Europe could match the United States in an Atlantic partnership. As he put it in the same Philadelphia speech: "The first order of business is for our European friends to go forward in forming the more perfect union which will some day soon make it" — that is, the Atlantic partnership — "possible". It is worth remembering that this is still the first order of business.

At the beginning of this lecture I spoke of the responsibility of the United States for much of world security. I know that I have not since done much to suggest how that loneliness can be shared. Of course it is less complete than is sometimes supposed. In Africa for example the interventions of the United States have so far been sporadic, and the task of helping African governments to prevent breakdowns of order has fallen with the exception of the Congo largely on Britain and France. In the Persian Gulf oil companies with large American interests operate in states whose stability has hitherto rested on British military protection. A major British military effort has succeeded in bringing to an end a serious quarrel between Indonesia and Malaysia. At the same time the United States presence in Vietnam undoubtedly helped to bring about a change internally in Indonesia which helped Britain in her task.

For Britain as for the United States overseas military expenditure is a heavy burden on our balance of payments. In the current year British net military expenditure in the Mediterranean, in the Middle East, and in the Far East is estimated at about 530 million dollars. Compare this with our recorded deficit across the exchanges in current expenditure and capital transactions in 1965, which was 893 million dollars, and you will see the impact of British military effort outside the continent of Europe on our balance of payments difficulties.

I doubt myself whether it is profitable to generalise in this field. What is clear is that Britain has existing commitments which have to be discharged and in my Party we believe we must discharge them. They cannot be suddenly abandoned unless either the threat which they are meant to meet has faded or some other way of meeting it has been found. Quite apart from arguments of good faith, the most expensive way of saving money is to pull troops out of a place before there are local forces able to provide protection against attack from outside and a local political structure which can resist subversion from within. The Congo is only now emerging from the slaughter and chaos which resulted from the sudden Belgian withdrawal in 1960 before those conditions were met. Seven years later we are urging the British Government not to expose Aden and South Arabia to a similar disaster.

There are some who conceive of a European policy for Britain as a withdrawal from all commitments outside Europe. I myself have never held that view. I have always believed that membership of the EEC would give us greater strength with which to continue to carry out these obligations. Indeed I go further than that. I would hope that Western Europe would in time come to carry out these obligations or some of them jointly as a European mission. That would best help to share any burden falling on the United

States provided that the New Europe and the United States could find a procedure for co-ordinating their policies more closely.

I turn now to the subject of European defence. Perhaps the simplest approach is to tackle in turn the three main European military powers and then if possible to identify a common European approach to defence.

Of the military powers, I take Britain first: a nuclear power buying a high and at present increasing proportion of her equipment from the United States, traditionally consulting the United States closely on all defence matters, at present preoccupied with the financial strain of her defence effort, in particular the burden across the exchanges of the forces which she maintains to carry out her commitments in Germany, the Middle East, and the Far East.

Next, France: Here I think there is a trap. The style of present French policy, particularly in military matters, is so clearly formed by President de Gaulle that we assume all too easily that the substance of the policy would not exist without him. I do not think this is right. It was not de Gaulle but the leaders of the Fourth Republic who laid the foundation of the French nuclear *force de frappe,* and all the evidence is that the present French Government's defence policy is broadly accepted by the French people. This is baffling to those who regard nationalism, particularly other people's nationalism, as irrational and out of date. But national feeling in France perhaps more than in any other country has lain at the root of French achievements, collective and individual. If this analysis is correct then it would be a mistake just to put a temporary roof over NATO to keep the worst of the weather out while we wait for the French to see their error and return to the integrated fold. We should on the contrary be working for a modernised alliance in which national loyalty and European loyalty as well as Atlantic loyalty can find an outlet. It is encouraging that the United States administration should have begun to move along this path in recent months, in particular by accepting the recommendation of the Committee of NATO Defence Ministers under Mr. McNamara's chairmanship that a Nuclear Planning Group be set up in NATO to share responsibilities which have hitherto tended to fall to the United States alone.

After France, Germany: Here I think we can see a radical change. In the first years after the war we dealt with a Western Germany politically powerless and economically in ruins. In recent years we have grown accustomed to dealing with a Germany which is economically powerful but politically passive and subdued. When I say "we" I include the French, Americans, and Russians with the British. This notable German passivity is partly the result of legal disabilities which survive from the immediate post-war period. But it stems mainly from the fact that the leaders of Western Germany in recent years have, whatever their differences, remained overwhelmingly conscious of the experience of the Third Reich and the disastrous effect which this had on Germany's standing in the world. Leaders are now coming to the front, backed by a new generation, who reject the idea that this experience should colour German policy for the rest of their lifetimes. We are now seeing a rapid sharpening of German foreign policy and a new determination to stand up for German interests, in defence as well as elsewhere. I noticed the account in the *New York Times* of the ministerial meeting of the North Atlantic Council last December. The correspondent wrote: "For the first time in the seventeen years since the founding of the Alliance a meeting of this kind was dominated not by the Americans but by the Germans." Since then the Germans have vociferously protested against the idea that they should sign without amendment a non-proliferation treaty negotiated between the Russians and the Americans. In 1963 they signed almost without protest the nuclear test ban treaty which had been negotiated in the same way. That is the measure of the change in Germany over three years.

This means a difficult adjustment for Western governments and some parts of Western public opinion. But even if we were able, which we are not, to persuade West Germany's new leaders to continue in the old cautious accepting ways the result would only be to increase the popular impatience registered in the minority vote for the extreme right in last autumn's local elections in Hesse and Bavaria. Some revival of German national feeling is inevitable; it is better that it should be felt through the moderate policies of democratically elected leaders than through the abuse of extremists.

The other countries of Western Europe, and in particular Italy, have a keen sense of the realities of military power which sometimes gives them clearer sight than their larger neighbours. For this reason they will not do anything in present circumstances to jeopardise the American commitment in Europe. On the other hand these are the countries most impatient with their national limitations and so most sympathetic with bold experiment on a European scale.

Can these different national attitudes be brought together into a European defence policy? In my view the question should be put the other way round. Can one conceive, over the long term, of a Europe growing together as we have described in an increasing number of ways and yet not trying to provide coherently for its own defence? I do not myself think it realistic to suppose that defence will be excluded indefinitely from the European experiment. Too many practical arguments point in the same direction. For example it is unlikely that after spending so much money and skill the

Governments of either Britain or France will simply allow their nuclear forces to wither away and return to complete reliance on the United States deterrent. Yet the cost of keeping a nuclear deterrent credible may well before long rise so far beyond the resources of any individual medium power, however determined, that the idea of a European defence system will prove highly attractive to them. Similarly we most of us recognise that the Russians and the East Europeans have a legitimate interest in ensuring that Germany does not emerge as an independent military power dominating Central Europe. Yet if what I have just said about Germany is right we are going to have to find a better means than we have now of assuring the Germans that they are equals in Europe and in the world. Here again logic points to an eventual European defence system.

This could not be an immediate proposal. The European experiment in unification would have to extend and consolidate itself over several years before it was ready to include defence. There would have to be greater progress in harmonising foreign policies than seems immediately possible. It is no use being too precise in advance. No one can predict what the exact practical content of a European defence system would then be. It would obviously begin with conventional forces and arms procurement. In my view it might also include a nuclear force based on the existing British and French forces which could be held in trusteeship for Europe as a whole. It is difficult to foresee developments further ahead. Similarly whether or not Western Europe would need its own antiballistic missile system cannot be predicted now. If these systems are developed we may be at the start of a new lap in the arms race between the United States and the USSR, the implications of which for the allies of either power cannot now be foreseen. The only point which I wish to make today is that the options should not be closed. Europe should be left free to crown its experiment in economic and political union with a defence system if at the time that is seen to be necessary.

At this point the labels become dangerous. If you mention a European defence system nowadays you are accused of being anti-American. How astonishing that accusation would have seemed fifteen years ago when the State Department was straining, perhaps overstraining itself to convert the old unhappy EDC from paper into fact. The trouble is of course that since then the idea has become linked in the popular mind with strong criticisms of American wisdom and reliability. It has been argued that Europe must provide for its own defence because the Americans cannot be trusted to risk nuclear war for the defence of Europe, or alternatively because the Americans cannot be trusted not to plunge Europe into an unnecessary war in defence of her non-European interests. I personally reject both these arguments. It is quite possible, and I believe sensible, to welcome the possibility of an eventual European defence system while upholding the American record in Europe and elsewhere. I have much sympathy with those Americans who ask why Europeans growing richer do not do more to look after their own defence. In overseas aid, trade, and investment I think the European record now compares well with the American; but in defence we Europeans are still very much the junior partners. It is not healthy that this balance should be so uneven. It is not healthy that every American troop movement in or out of Germany should be reported in apocalyptic terms in the European press. It is not healthy that so many educated Europeans look upon everything to do with nuclear weapons as a complicated and slightly disreputable business with which, thanks to the Americans, they need not soil their minds. It is not healthy that the Americans and Russians, as a natural result of their nuclear pre-eminence, should discuss privately matters such as a non-proliferation treaty which intimately affect the security of Europe. The present United States administration has shown itself conscious of this uneven balance, in Mr. McNamara's work in NATO, in President Johnson's speech in New York in October of 1966, and on other occasions. I believe that legitimate concern for American interests would lead any American administration positively to support a European defence system, provided that it was sensibly constructed and compatible with America's own defence effort.

These are important provisos, which would have to be met through the Atlantic Alliance. The metaphor of the two pillars is well-worn but still serves its purpose as well as any. If we conceive of NATO and the Alliance as resting on the two columns of the American and the European military efforts, our present troubles are caused by the weakness of the European pillar. It needs binding together and building up, not necessarily to the height of the American pillar, but enough to carry a fair share of the weight. But what should the alliance itself consist of? The present position, in which the alliance means one thing to fourteen of its members, and something quite different to the fifteenth, France, is clearly very difficult. I do not myself agree with the thesis that the Atlantic Alliance should be based as closely as possible on the traditional European alliances of the nineteenth century — that is, that it should consist primarily of a commitment to come to each other's help in case of attack but should not include common preparation against such attack. That was a workable thesis when mobilising for war could be done on a national scale. Today, to take one example, the Atlantic Alliance to remain credible needs a fully automated system of early warning against surprise air attack. From the first bleep over the radar as the enemy aircraft or missiles are registered, through the whole data processing down to the order to aircraft or missile to fire on the intruders, the process can be fully automatic. National frontiers are of course irrelevant to this. The contract for the system, called NADGE, was awarded a few months ago; it is significant that France is one of the countries taking part. There is, I think, from the political point of view a parallel here between what has happened in the EEC and in NATO. In both, practical needs are a signpost showing the way out of theoretical dispute. The theoretical dispute goes on. It is no use expecting France to go back on her arguments against supra-nationalism in economics and welcome the European Commission or the European Parliament as arbiters of her essential economic interests; but the logic of daily practical and technical decisions leads France as well as her partners to widen the scope of the Community's action. Similarly it is no use expecting France to go back on her arguments against supra-nationalism in defence, and again place her fighting units in peace-time under the command of American Generals; but the advance of technology convinces France that a highly integrated project like NADGE is necessary for her safety. Planners and service chiefs, discussing their practical needs, should be able to keep the present breach in NATO within reasonable bounds. I believe myself that it is likely to be healed eventually when a European defence system is ready to work out with its North American partners a new and more rational division of effort.

I have deliberately left to last the discussion of Communism and our relations with Communist powers. In the last twenty years there has been a divergence in the popular analysis of the Soviet danger on either side of the Atlantic. The Europeans have tended to assume too quickly that Soviet policy has changed permanently and that tough but basically rational and peaceable technocrats are securely in charge. This was widely assumed in 1955 before Hungary, and in 1961 before Cuba; it is assumed again in 1967. Of course there is evidence of a Soviet shift of policy, of an increased desire for consumer goods, and increased reluctance to risk war, a gradual gain of intellectual freedom. The trend is undoubtedly there, but trends can be interrupted or even reversed for considerable periods by some mischance or vigorous personality. On the other hand it would be fair to say that in the United States there has been an opposite tendency to attribute too much weight to the Communists in the world as a whole. The world would be disorderly in 1967 even if there were no Communists. The rise of new states, new techniques, new expectations, all rising faster than the resources to satisfy them, would see to that.

What is the right analysis of the Communist world today? We see two sets of leaders, the Soviet and the Chinese, each interested both in conserving the power of themselves and their people and in spreading their brand of Communism in the non-Communist world. One set, the Soviet leaders, have increasingly found a contradiction between these two aims. They have not publicly renounced their aim of spreading Communism, but they have restricted the means which they use. They have found that expansion of the Communist world by military means would require a concentration of resources on military expenditure which might shake their hold on their people and, more important, that it would risk the destruction in nuclear war of all the achievements of the Soviet state. They have found that the prosperity of the Soviet state can be increased by trading with the West and now in particular by encouraging the West to set up whole factories in the Soviet Union. They have similarly found that the security of the Soviet state can be increased by reaching limited agreements with the West, for example the recent agreement for a treaty on outer space and the 1963 partial nuclear test ban. This policy of trade and limited political agreement is, of course, combined with a policy of political and economic sapping of Western positions, particularly in the underdeveloped world. As I said before, the policy could be temporarily changed by some chance gust of wind in the other direction; but the trend is clear.

The Chinese leaders on the other hand have found no contradiction between preserving their own power and proclaiming that all means of spreading Communism are legitimate. They have of course usually proclaimed rather than openly acted. Their intervention in Korea was a response to the North Korean defeat. Their invasion of India was a carefully limited exercise in humiliating a rival. Their support for Hanoi consists largely of food, small arms, technicians, railway equipment, and of course transit rights for Soviet material through Chinese territory. They have not, so far, sent volunteers into Vietnam. The Chinese are remarkably passive in face of Marshall Chiang Kai Shek's survival on Taiwan and the offshore islands. There is no reason to find here a comforting contrast between Chinese words and deeds and conclude that they do not mean the terrifying things which they say. The fact is that the Chinese are short on power. The question is whether by the time they are long on power — that is, when they have nuclear capacity and a developed economic base — the aims of their revolution will have changed. It used to be supposed that this point would be reached in the 1980s. I know there are some who now doubt whether this is the right analysis, who conclude from the latest convulsions in China that she will either lurch back into the chaos of the 1920s or shut herself up as a hermit state, malevolent but so chronically weak that we need not worry about her ill-will. I doubt myself if this is right. Certainly what is happening now in

China will put back the moment when she reaches the level of power which I have described. But the energy and ingenuity of the Chinese and their capacity for disciplined sacrifice have been proved too often to be entirely discounted. It looks as if the fire-fighters in China — the officials and technicians who want to protect the real achievements of the Peoples' Republic — have managed to get the flames of the cultural revolution under control. It would be sensible to assume that before the end of the century China will have achieved the economic and nuclear proficiency of a major power.

Faced with this situation the Western response should be twofold: to prevent the spread of Communism and to influence the character of the Soviet and Chinese Revolutions. I have said enough about preventing the spread; but can we hope to influence the character of the two Revolutions? Probably in the case of China only marginally. Certainly it would be rash to assume that anything the West could reasonably do in its relations with China would have a decisive effect on Chinese policy. That does not mean that we should not do what we can. There are surely good arguments for placing clearly on the Chinese the onus of their own isolation, leaving it to them to refuse to exchange Ambassadors or to take their seat at the UN except under manifestly unreasonable conditions. I am sure there are good arguments for expanding trade with China and indeed all Communist countries to the limit of commercial prudence. There is no need to press businessmen in this direction; they have found almost all Communist countries to be good payers and reliable suppliers.

There is still, I know, a feeling that to trade with Communists is to give them an unrequited addition of strength. Of course the Western partner in the trade would also on the same argument gain strength. But quite apart from this point, the argument against trading in non-strategic commodities is really an argument in favour of a policy which no one follows wholeheartedly, a policy of destroying revolution by economic sanctions. Economic sanctions are a notoriously unreliable weapon against anyone (we are seeing that today in Rhodesia), and evasion grows easier as world trade becomes more complicated. Experience suggests that against a revolutionary regime sanctions drive the revolution in on itself, making its policies harsher and more dangerous. If you calculate that you can destroy a hostile regime by these means it may not matter that in the meantime it becomes more hostile. But if, as in the case of China, you clearly cannot destroy the revolutionary regime by refusing to trade with it, then surely the greatest possible trade in non-strategic goods should be encouraged.

Foreign trade means foreign contracts and an interest in foreign methods and foreign goods. It may stimulate the appetite and lead to impatience with a system which denies choice to the consumer. I believe that contacts through trade could do more to influence the character of the Chinese Revolution than diplomatic contacts at Peking or the UN. Of course foreign trade helps the Chinese Communist leaders in the sense that it makes the Chinese people a very little more prosperous; but if we are interested as we should be in a change in the character of the Chinese Revolution, then this is also a help to ourselves. There are no reliable figures, but it is certain that the Sino-Soviet dispute has led to a drastic fall in Soviet exports and an end to Soviet technical assistance to China. The West must take sides in the Sino-Soviet dispute in the sense that the West obviously favours co-existence. But I suggest that the West should not side with the Soviet Union to the extent of renouncing the opportunities for influencing the character of the Chinese revolution which the Soviet withdrawal from China has created. Last year the British held an exhibition of scientific instruments in Tientsin and the French have a similar exhibition in Shanghai. This is the type of initiative which in its own interests the West should encourage. I know that there is a limit to the possible expansion of China's foreign trade, particularly in manufactured goods and equipment, so long as she has to import between 5 and 6 million tons of foodgrains annually at a cost of some 400 million dollars. But her total foreign trade in 1965 was about 3.4 billion dollars, and already three fifths of it was with non-Communist countries.

Finally we come to the Soviet Union and to the states of Eastern Europe. Here there is clearly a bigger role for Western Europe. Western Europe as a whole and the EEC in particular have proved to have a strong attractive power for their neighbours to the East. This has happened I think for two reasons. First, the rapid rise in the standard of living in Western Europe, coinciding with the development of the EEC, has helped to stimulate psychologically a demand for consumer goods in Eastern Europe. Second, the accent placed in the West on European unity has encouraged the East European states to feel that they have a part to play as Europeans and not simply as the permanent subordinates of the Soviet Union. This attractive power of Western Europe should be maintained and developed. There is a limit to what can be done by extending institutions; the idea of extending the EEC immediately to include the states of Eastern Europe is put forward only by those who wish to make the EEC unrecognisable. The Council of Europe and the GATT require qualifications for full membership which are difficult for states with centrally directed economies to fulfil. Nevertheless, progress has been made with associating Eastern European countries, particularly Yugoslavia, with projects of these two organisations.

There is much more scope for expanding trade. Here the emphasis is now on the supply of whole factories by the West. Last year there was the agreement to establish a Fiat automobile plant in the Soviet Union. This year two British companies, Leylands and BMH, have put in similar proposals. There have been many other examples. In such deals the difficulty is one of credit. The supplier has to organise fiance, usually drawn from a range of private and public institutions, and the government of the supplier has to decide whether the credit extended goes beyond what is commercially reasonable. There used to be much controversy about this in the days when I was the British Minister responsible, and we were sometimes roughly criticised for wanting to go too far. Luckily yesterday's heresy is today's orthodoxy, and credits over a reasonable term are now normal. I was glad to notice that in his speech of October 7, 1966, President Johnson announced that the Export-Import Bank was prepared to finance American exports for the Soviet-Italian Fiat plant on a long-term basis.

The question of German unity stands as a roadblock in Europe, limiting the scope of almost all important projects and contacts between East and West. In his Statement to the Bundestag in December 1966 the German Chancellor, Dr. Kiesinger, took a considerable step forward. He abandoned so far as Eastern European states were concerned the doctrine that West Germany could not establish diplomatic relations with states which recognised the East German regime. Roumania has responded by exchanging Ambassadors; despite the angry opposition of the East German regime, other East European countries may follow suit.

The Germans have in the last twenty years looked to the four powers which divided Germany to bring the division to an end. There are still some who expect German reunification to come about through a four-power agreement. But I think most Germans now realise that the obstacles are too great along that path and that they must seek a more hopeful remedy, such as that sketched by Chancellor Kiesinger in the speech to which I have referred. He said: "We wish to do our utmost to prevent the two parts of our nation from drifting apart as long as the country is divided; we wish to ease the situation, not harden it; we wish to bridge the gulfs, not deepen them. That is why we wish to do all we can to encourage human, economic, and cultural relations with our countrymen in the other part of Germany". Here again in East Germany is a regime whose character has to change before there can be a political answer to the problem which it presents. I am not sure that the NATO powers have so far drawn the logical conclusion from Chancellor Kiesinger's speech. The contacts of other NATO countries with East Germany, circumscribed for so long for valid political reasons, should be systematically expanded now that the West German Government itself has marked this as the path to follow.

Our other task is to meet the fear of revived German military strength which still dominates the political thinking of Eastern Europe. I have talked recently with Mr. Kosygin and with the Polish Foreign Minster, Mr. Rapacki. I know how deeply they still feel about Germany. Yet we have to reassure them without imposing on Germany servitudes of a kind which will simply breed the type of violent German nationalism which the East Europeans most fear. Chancellor Kiesinger has renounced for Germany national control and national ownership of nuclear weapons. The Soviet Union says this is not enough. But no other line of argument remains, once it is accepted that if you try to discriminate permanently against Germany you breed more dangers than you cure. It seems to me that we can only strengthen the argument by expanding the scope and membership of the EEC to include Britain and binding the new Germany ever more closely together with the other European partners. Only at that stage then will there be achieved that opinion in Eastern Europe, and indeed in much of Western Europe, which would accept that the risks involved in solving the German problem, removing the roadblock in the middle of Europe, would be worth the taking.

Twenty years ago there were compelling reasons for bringing about the greater unity of Europe. Sir Winston Churchill when he was launching the great United Europe movement saw Europe as "a rubble heap, a charnel-house, a breeding ground of pestilence and hate". That was only twenty years ago. The very survival of the people of Western Europe depended on some form of unity being achieved. Western Europe survived. Many factors contributed to this, not least the massive generosity of the United States. The hunger and the cold that ravaged the peoples of a war-torn continent have been largely eliminated. And yet I believe that survival remains the driving force behind the desire for wider European unity. Europe today fights for the survival not of past glories, but for the heritage of ideals and the inheritance of skills which can enrich our society, and can help build the world of tomorrow. Europe seeks to survive as an economic entity, not in order to gorge its appetites or satisfy its lusts, but so that Europe can contribute to the ever rising standards of peoples all over the world and help fulfil the needs of the hungry and the homeless in those less fortunate parts of the globe that still lie in the shadow of want. Europe seeks to survive as a political entity, not in order to preserve illusions of power, but so as to contribute a solid pillar upon which world security can be built and on which world peace may rest. A Europe that remains disintegrated could create a chasm that could swallow up the great powers of the East and West and leave the uncommitted world in darkness. But a Europe united and strong can become a catalyst for that even wider unity on which rest the hopes of those still enslaved, a unity which remains the inspiration of the free peoples of the world.

Index